A Kid's Winter EcoJournal

With Nature Activities for Exploring the Season

Toni Albert

Designed and Illustrated by

Margaret Brandt

Trickle Creek Books

"Teaching Kids to Care for the Earth"

Tel: 717-766-2638 • 800-353-2791 • Fax: 717-766-1343

www.TrickleCreekBooks.com

Author's Acknowledgments

Thank you, Bob Albert, for our home at Trickle Creek,
for clearing the land and building the house with your own hands,
for long happy walks in the woods, and long happy days together.
Thank you for being my computerman!

Thank you, Pat Van Etten, for power-prayers and unselfed love.
Aren't we having fun growing Trickle Creek Books?

Thank you, Margaret, for letting your love of nature
shine through every beautiful page of art.

Artist's Acknowledgments

I'd like to dedicate this art to all of the special people
who teach and inspire through the visual arts.
May your dedication and enthusiasm be reflected in these pages.

Dedication

To all of the children and all of their teachers who love to explore
the strange and wonderful wildernesses in backyards.
To Avery in the winter of her birth.

Copyright © 1998 by Toni Albert
All rights reserved
Printed in the United States of America on recycled paper
First Edition

First printing 1998, Second printing 2005

Publisher's Cataloging in Publication
(Prepared by Quality Books Inc.)
Albert, Toni.
    A kid's winter ecojournal : with nature activities for
exploring the seasons / Toni Albert ; illustrated and designed
by Margaret Brandt.
    p. cm.
    SUMMARY: Includes tips on writing about nature, short
entries from the author's nature journal, and nature activities for
exploring the season.
    Preassigned LCCN: 96-61932
    ISBN-13: 9780964074262
    ISBN-10: 1-9640742-6-5
    1. Nature study–Juvenile literature. 2. Natural history–
Juvenile literature. 3. Ecology–Juvenile literature. 4. Winter–
Juvenile literature. 5. Diaries–Authorship–Juvenile literature.
I. Title.

QH48.A535 1998   574.5'43

            QB197-40116

Published in the United States by Trickle Creek Books
500 Andersontown Road, Mechanicsburg, PA 17055

All of the nature activities in this book should be done with
proper supervision from a responsible adult. The publisher
is not responsible for accidents or injuries that may occur
when children explore the natural world.

Contents

Introduction
Writing About Nature

When snow and ice cover the Earth, all of nature appears to be sleeping. In winter, it takes a little more looking and a little more listening to discover signs of wildlife. But winter is a wonderful time to learn how to follow animal tracks or to recognize the call of a lone bird or to spot the berries on a bush. After you've braved the cold to explore a wintry landscape, it's good to be inside again, snug and warm. Long winter evenings are perfect for reading a good book—or for writing one! You can keep a winter eco-journal, a personal nature journal, just as I do.

What should you write in your eco-journal?
Anything about nature…

- Write daily notes about the way the season progresses. This takes careful observation. For example, did you ever notice when the ground freezes or which birds migrate or where icicles form?

- Write a poem, a story, or an essay. Draw inspiration from the whine of wind rushing through leafless trees or from the faint, sweet fragrance of bittersweet berries or from the silence of glittering stars on a frozen night. Express your thoughts and feelings about nature.

- Make quick field notes when you are observing something outside. Record details that you may forget later—the colors of a bird, the pattern of tracks across a snowy field, the size and shape of ice needles on a pond, the activity of a squirrel. Field notes often include the date and time, the weather, and the location, as well as a description of what you were observing and what happened to it while you were watching. (You can make quick drawings, too.)

- Use your field notes to write a careful description of what you observed. Use detailed, descriptive language.

- Keep a record of an interesting nature study or experiment, such as exploring beneath the snow, finding out what foods birds like best, or testing snow to see if it is polluted.

- Write an interview with a park ranger, a wildlife rehabilitator, a zookeeper, or someone who knows something special about wildlife or wildlands.

- Write a report about an animal or plant that interests you.

- Keep a nature diary with descriptions of special events, such as spotting an owl or hiking in a blizzard.

- Read a book about nature. Then write your response.

Keeping an eco-journal will give you a chance to write from your own direct experience. (And writing based on experience is often your best writing.) It is easy to draw inspiration from nature. As you write in your eco-journal, you may find yourself painting word pictures and making your writing sound like poetry. Writing about nature will help you learn to be more observant and to enjoy nature more, too.

Exploring Nature

It's fun to run through a field, scramble up rocks, crash through the underbrush, or splash in a creek. But that's not the best way to see wildlife. You need to learn to enter the quiet world of animals and plants slowly and gently without disturbing them. You must practice being still—but with all your senses alert. You must become observant and more observant and more and more observant! Then you'll see where a chipmunk enters its burrow. Or spot a fox trotting through a field. Or discover what animal lives in a den tree. It takes patience and skill to explore nature, but the delight of discovery and the joy of caring for our Earth will last all of your life.

Here are some tips for exploring nature:

- In winter, wear layers of warm clothing. Protect your hands, feet, face and head with warm outerwear. Don't wear cotton. Wool, especially wool socks, will keep you warmer and drier.

- Be prepared. Bring drinking water or a hot drink, plastic containers for collecting specimens, a magnifying lens, and a notebook and pencil. If you have a camera, binoculars, or field guides, bring them, too. Bring a small trash bag for litter.

- In winter, carry a high-energy trail mix made of chocolate, dried fruit, and nuts. Eating a high-calorie snack will help keep you warm and give you energy. Remember, you can get very tired when walking in deep snow.

- Look for animals at dawn or dusk. That's when you will be most likely to see them.

- Move quietly. Sit still in one place for awhile—at least five minutes. Hide partly behind a tree or boulder. Try to feel like a part of nature.

- Don't put your hands into hollow logs or trees before you look inside.

- Use all of your senses. Listen to the sounds around you. Breathe deeply and notice different smells. Look around you and observe details. Touch the bark of trees, fuzzy moss, crunchy snow. Taste edible plants and berries *only* when an adult gives you permission. (Some plants are poisonous.) Don't forget to use your sense of wonder, too!

- Look for signs of wildlife: animal tracks, animal trails, burrows, nests, feathers or fur, bones, droppings, and evidence that animals have eaten or grazed (squirrels drop nutshells, rabbits strip leaves from small plants, birds take berries from bushes).

- If you see an animal and want to get closer, don't approach it directly. Take a roundabout route, walking slowly and steadily. Don't look the animal in the eye or you will alarm it. The best way to get a closer look at an animal is with binoculars.

- Always leave an area as clean as you found it—or cleaner.

Special tips on winter safety:

- NEVER walk on ice unless it has been officially declared safe. When the air temperature is below freezing or when the wind chill factor is especially high, don't stay outside too long and don't go too far from home. Watch for signs of frostbite. If your skin feels prickly or numb, go inside.

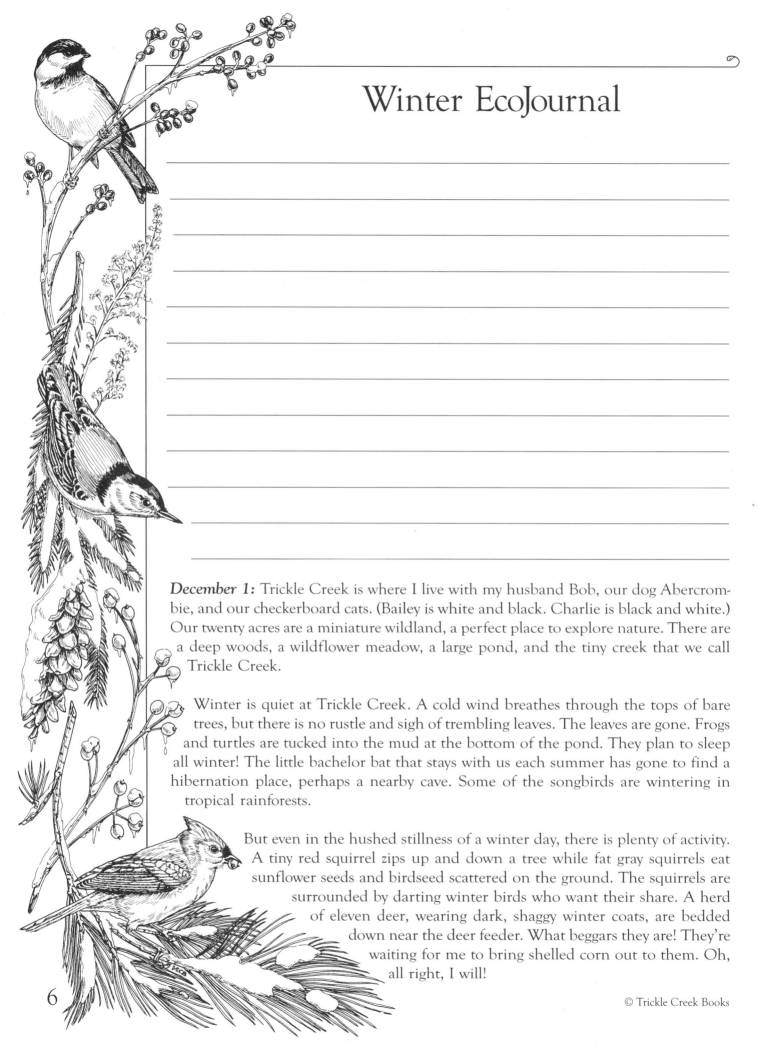

Winter EcoJournal

_____

_____

_____

_____

_____

_____

_____

_____

_____

_____

_____

_____

December 1: Trickle Creek is where I live with my husband Bob, our dog Abercrombie, and our checkerboard cats. (Bailey is white and black. Charlie is black and white.) Our twenty acres are a miniature wildland, a perfect place to explore nature. There are a deep woods, a wildflower meadow, a large pond, and the tiny creek that we call Trickle Creek.

Winter is quiet at Trickle Creek. A cold wind breathes through the tops of bare trees, but there is no rustle and sigh of trembling leaves. The leaves are gone. Frogs and turtles are tucked into the mud at the bottom of the pond. They plan to sleep all winter! The little bachelor bat that stays with us each summer has gone to find a hibernation place, perhaps a nearby cave. Some of the songbirds are wintering in tropical rainforests.

But even in the hushed stillness of a winter day, there is plenty of activity. A tiny red squirrel zips up and down a tree while fat gray squirrels eat sunflower seeds and birdseed scattered on the ground. The squirrels are surrounded by darting winter birds who want their share. A herd of eleven deer, wearing dark, shaggy winter coats, are bedded down near the deer feeder. What beggars they are! They're waiting for me to bring shelled corn out to them. Oh, all right, I will!

6

Trickle Creek

There is an undeniable excitement when the first winter snowflakes fall on earth like powdered sugar on a cake. Snow and ice transform the world into a magical wonderland of soft sounds and white mounds. Although in winter there is less animal activity—and certainly less plant activity—it is still an interesting season to explore. On one hand, you will need to be especially observant to find any sign of wildlife or plant life. You'll have to listen carefully for a lone bird call or look beneath the snow for green moss or search a tree for interesting shelf mushrooms. On the other hand, some signs are more obvious in winter—animal tracks in the snow, squirrel nests in trees, bright berries, or fluttering, chattering birds at a feeder.

One of the best ways to learn about nature—and start to really care about it—is to visit the same place over and over through all the seasons until you know it by heart. The place can be your backyard or school yard, a vacant lot or city park, a nature trail or country path, or even a single tree rising above city pavement. It's fun to make a map or drawing—perhaps a view from the air—of the place you choose to observe. You can make notes on your map to record seasonal changes, wildlife sightings, and sources of water, food, and shelter for wildlife. It's fun to "keep track of tracks" during the winter by following animal tracks and trails and then drawing them on your map. Try to identify the tracks, and add sketches of animals to your map, too. (*See page 35, "Tracking Animals in Snow."*)

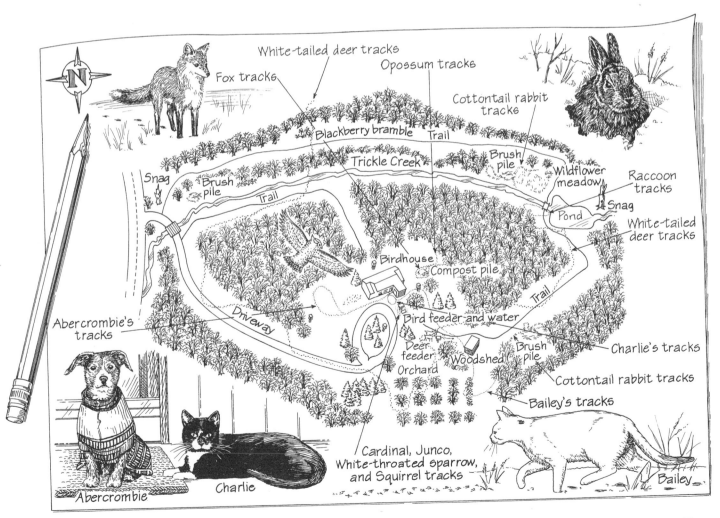

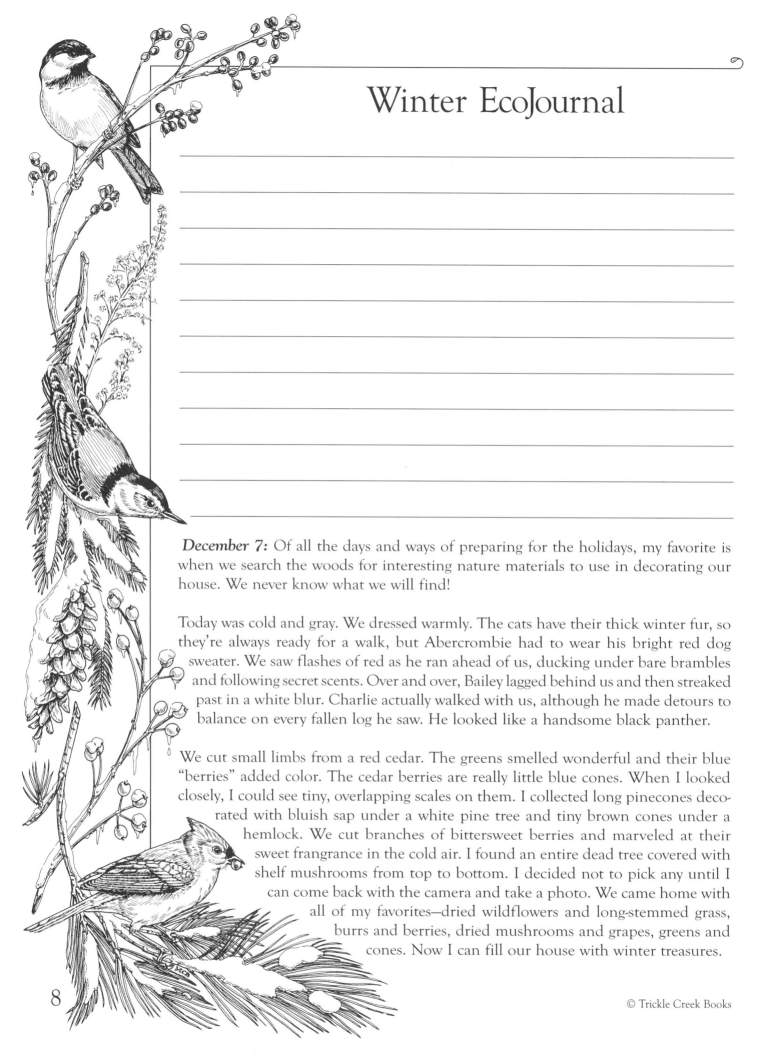

Winter EcoJournal

_____

_____

_____

_____

_____

_____

_____

_____

_____

_____

_____

_____

_____

_____

December 7: Of all the days and ways of preparing for the holidays, my favorite is when we search the woods for interesting nature materials to use in decorating our house. We never know what we will find!

Today was cold and gray. We dressed warmly. The cats have their thick winter fur, so they're always ready for a walk, but Abercrombie had to wear his bright red dog sweater. We saw flashes of red as he ran ahead of us, ducking under bare brambles and following secret scents. Over and over, Bailey lagged behind us and then streaked past in a white blur. Charlie actually walked with us, although he made detours to balance on every fallen log he saw. He looked like a handsome black panther.

We cut small limbs from a red cedar. The greens smelled wonderful and their blue "berries" added color. The cedar berries are really little blue cones. When I looked closely, I could see tiny, overlapping scales on them. I collected long pinecones decorated with bluish sap under a white pine tree and tiny brown cones under a hemlock. We cut branches of bittersweet berries and marveled at their sweet frangrance in the cold air. I found an entire dead tree covered with shelf mushrooms from top to bottom. I decided not to pick any until I can come back with the camera and take a photo. We came home with all of my favorites—dried wildflowers and long-stemmed grass, burrs and berries, dried mushrooms and grapes, greens and cones. Now I can fill our house with winter treasures.

8

Wonderful Winter Leftovers

At first glance, a winter landscape looks bleak and uninteresting. Much of what gives color and excitement to other seasons is gone. There are no flowers covered with butterflies and insects, no turtles in the grass or frogs at the pond, no leaves on the trees. But with close observation, you may be surprised at what is left.

Plan a winter walk to gather "winter leftovers." Look for anything that catches your eye in the black-and-white world of winter. You may find clusters of plump blue-black berries on privet shrubs, deep red rose hips on wild rose bushes, bright red holly berries, or leftover bittersweet berries that still smell sweet. Look for wild grape vines where you can collect curly wooden tendrils and tiny bunches of dried grapes that have fallen to the ground. Pick up pinecones, nutshells, or dried seed-pods. Carefully pull shelf mushrooms from dead trees or fallen logs. Gather dried wildflowers and fluffy weeds that are still standing. All of these natural materials are perfect for making holiday wreaths and arrangements.

To keep the materials you gather from getting tangled or crushed, build a collecting caddy to take with you on your walk. You will need six 11.5-ounce coffee cans and a scrap piece of a two-by-four about 16 inches long. To make a handle for the caddy, attach two screw eyes about 8 inches apart on a narrow edge of the two-by-four. Thread a length of rope through the screw eyes and knot the rope on each end. (Another way to make a handle is to nail part of an old belt to the narrow edge of the two-by-four.) Lay each can on a piece of scrap wood and punch a hole in the side of the can with a long nail or a scratch awl. The hole should be about ½ inch from the top of the can. Then attach three cans to each side of the two-by-four with short screws about ¾ inch long. Keep the tops of the cans flush with the top edge of the two-by-four. You'll enjoy using your collecting caddy all year long.

Dried fox grapes

Winter leftovers are great for making holiday decorations!

Wild grape tendrils

Nutshell

Rope handle threaded through screw eyes

Shelf mushroom

Pinecone

Coffee cans attached to caddy with screws

16-inch piece of two-by-four

Winged seeds

It's easy to make a "collecting caddy" with coffee cans.

Winter EcoJournal

_____

_____

_____

_____

_____

_____

_____

_____

_____

_____

_____

_____

_____

_____

_____

_____

_____

December 10: What a wonderful day to be inside! It's been raining for two days and off and on for weeks before that. I've never seen the woods so wet. The trails are slippery mud. Some trails have become streambeds with water gushing down them and more water cutting across them. The pond is overflowing its banks and washing duckweed onto the grass. Big, brown, soggy sycamore leaves line our driveway. The wet sounds of spattering rain and dripping water and gurgling streams have continued hour after hour. By 4:30 in the afternoon, this dark day had turned to night.

My daughter Sandi and I spent the evening making Christmas wreathes in Bob's workshop. It's warm and cozy there. Charlie found a box to sleep in while we worked, but Bailey insisted on going outside. Fifteen minutes later, we heard him urgently scratching at the window, admitting that he had made a mistake. We dried him off with a towel. He likes to be scrubbed, and that made him purr. On a miserable night like this, most of the animals in the woods have found shelter. But when I looked out at the compost pile before going to bed, there was a sopping-wet, bedraggled opossum eating the leftovers from our dinner.

Make a Nature Wreath

To make an outstanding nature wreath, gather all of the interesting natural materials that you can find on a winter walk. (*See page 9, "Wonderful Winter Leftovers."*) Find a large work space or big table, and lay the materials out where you can see them.

I usually buy a fresh wreath made of several kinds of greens, such as pine, spruce, and cedar. But you can cut small branches from evergreens and make your own wreath. Simply bend a coat hanger into a circle with the curved hanger at the top. Tie the greens to the circle with short lengths of string or florist's wire. Keep adding greens until your wreath is fat and full.

Once you have a wreath, you are ready to have fun decorating it with the materials you gathered. The easiest way to attach the materials to the wreath is with a hot glue gun, although white glue or wire will work, too. If you use a hot glue gun, ask an adult to show you how to use it safely, and have the adult stay with you while you work. The glue gun and the glue get very hot!

First glue (or wire) the bigger things—like pinecones, shelf mushrooms, and nuts or nutshells—to the wreath. Don't place all of the big things together. Space them in a pleasing way around the wreath. Then add bright clusters of berries. Hold several stems of berries together, put glue on the stems, and poke them into the wreath. Then add dry weeds and flowers to fill in empty spaces. Keep working until the wreath is filled with interesting and beautiful details. Finally add a big bow. If you hang your nature wreath outside in the cold, it should last through February!

Be creative when you make a nature wreath. Add anything natural—burrs, nutshells, dried mushrooms—anything!

When I was a child, I made wreaths like this to sell. Everybody loved them!

Florist's wire

Glue gun

Winter EcoJournal

December 12: In winter when food is scarce, the deer check the deer feeder several times a day. Today I watched a small herd eating together. With their muzzles in the corn and their ears pulled back, they looked like little fuzzy donkeys. There were small commotions when the fawns tried to push their way up to the feeder, but for the most part, the deer are gentle and polite.

One doe boldly left the herd to eat the corn that was scattered on the ground for the birds. She knew I was standing at the window not twenty feet away, but she seemed perfectly at ease. As she nuzzled the kernels of corn, I could see a white halo of whiskers around her nose. I saw her soft white belly, her thin-stick legs, and her dark-rimmed, velvety ears. How beautiful she is! When the herd had eaten every kernel of corn, they moved together into the woods, and she bounded off to join them.

Make More Winter Wonders

Once you have gathered all of the winter leftovers you can find—and after you have practiced making a nature wreath—use your imagination to make other winter wonders. Make a special Yule log by decorating a short log with natural materials. Begin by carefully digging up a "mat" of green moss. (Moss grows so low to the ground that cold winds don't disturb it, and it often stays green all winter.) Shake the loose dirt from the moss roots, but keep the moss in good-sized mats. Apply hot glue or white glue directly to the dirty underside of the moss, and glue the moss to the top of the log. Then glue berries, pinecones, greens, and other materials to the log. Add a bright bow if you like. The log can be kept indoors or outdoors as a unique holiday decoration.

Another easy way to enjoy the winter materials you collect is to make a big bowl or jar of potpourri (pronounced *po-pu-ree'*). Potpourri is usually a mixture of dried flowers, herbs, and spices that smell good. You can make a wonderful mixture of pine sprigs, winter berries, small pinecones, seedpods, and dried flowers. Add cinnamon sticks or dried orange peel for fragrance. Or buy scented oil—perhaps orange, cinnamon, or pine—at a craft store. On a cold winter day when the frozen air is pure and odorless, it's fun to go inside and smell cinnamon and pine!

If you find a hollow log with a hole in its side, it's fun to put greens in it.

Unusual Yule Logs

Pine oil

Orange oil

A little bag of homemade potpourri makes a great gift!

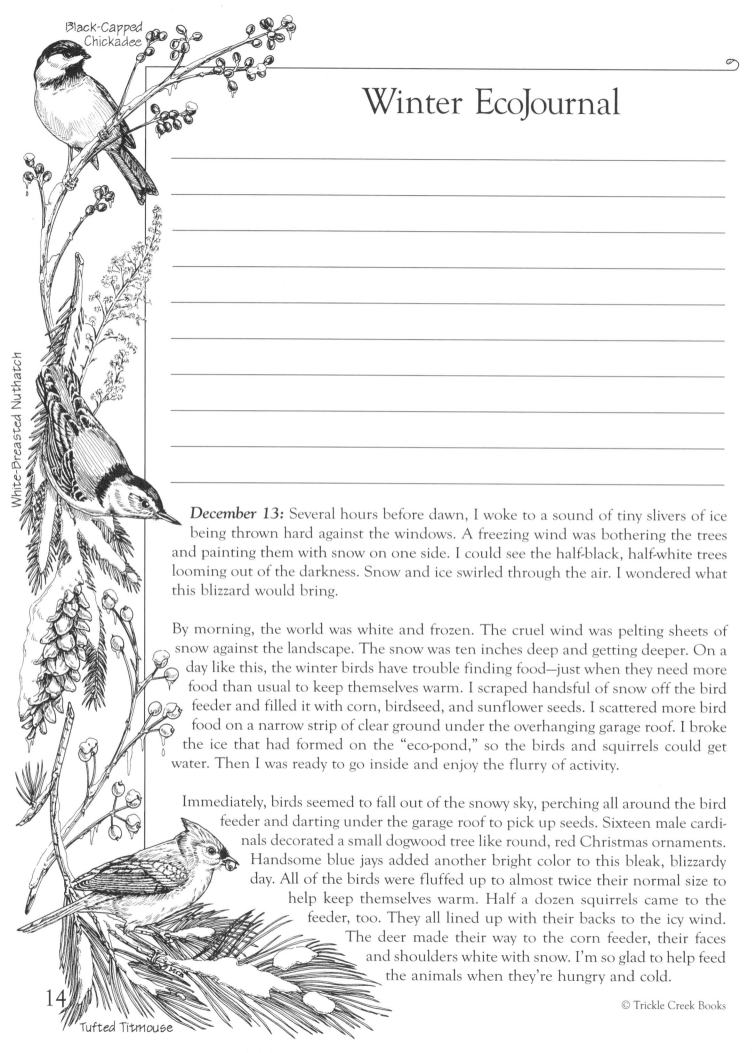

Black-Capped
Chickadee

White-Breasted Nuthatch

Winter EcoJournal

_____

_____

_____

_____

_____

_____

_____

_____

_____

_____

_____

December 13: Several hours before dawn, I woke to a sound of tiny slivers of ice being thrown hard against the windows. A freezing wind was bothering the trees and painting them with snow on one side. I could see the half-black, half-white trees looming out of the darkness. Snow and ice swirled through the air. I wondered what this blizzard would bring.

By morning, the world was white and frozen. The cruel wind was pelting sheets of snow against the landscape. The snow was ten inches deep and getting deeper. On a day like this, the winter birds have trouble finding food—just when they need more food than usual to keep themselves warm. I scraped handsful of snow off the bird feeder and filled it with corn, birdseed, and sunflower seeds. I scattered more bird food on a narrow strip of clear ground under the overhanging garage roof. I broke the ice that had formed on the "eco-pond," so the birds and squirrels could get water. Then I was ready to go inside and enjoy the flurry of activity.

Immediately, birds seemed to fall out of the snowy sky, perching all around the bird feeder and darting under the garage roof to pick up seeds. Sixteen male cardinals decorated a small dogwood tree like round, red Christmas ornaments. Handsome blue jays added another bright color to this bleak, blizzardy day. All of the birds were fluffed up to almost twice their normal size to help keep themselves warm. Half a dozen squirrels came to the feeder, too. They all lined up with their backs to the icy wind. The deer made their way to the corn feeder, their faces and shoulders white with snow. I'm so glad to help feed the animals when they're hungry and cold.

14

Tufted Titmouse

Build an Observation Bird Feeder

If you have a bird feeder in your yard, you can easily observe the birds that come to it. But an even better way to watch birds is to attach an observation bird feeder directly to your window. Then, as birds feed, you can look them right in the eye and really get to know them!

To make an observation feeder, you will need a piece of exterior grade plywood, ½"x2"x24"x24". Using the layout below, cut out the parts of the feeder with a handsaw or jigsaw. Remove any splinters with coarse sandpaper. To attach the bottom of the feeder to the sides, use a drill to make pilot holes smaller than the diameter of the nail you use. (Plywood will split if you don't pre-drill the holes.) Then nail the bottom to the sides. At a building supply store, buy a ⅛"-x-12"-x-26" piece of plexiglass for the roof. Drill two ¼" holes in the plexiglass, so that they line up with the sides of the feeder. Hammer 4-penny finish nails through the holes and into the top edges of the sides to keep the roof from slipping off. (You will be able to lift the roof off to put birdseed in the feeder.) You can also install a basket made of ½" wire mesh to hold suet. Just nail or staple the basket into place.

The way you position the observation feeder in a window will depend on the type of window you have. If you have an exterior window sill that extends outwards, simply nail the bottom of the feeder into the sill. Then use a wedge-shaped diagonal brace against the house. Attach the brace to the feeder with screws. You don't need to attach the brace to the house. If your window doesn't have a sill, you will need to attach a strip of wood to the house siding. Then you can nail the bottom of the feeder to the strip and attach a diagonal brace below it. (See the illustration below.)

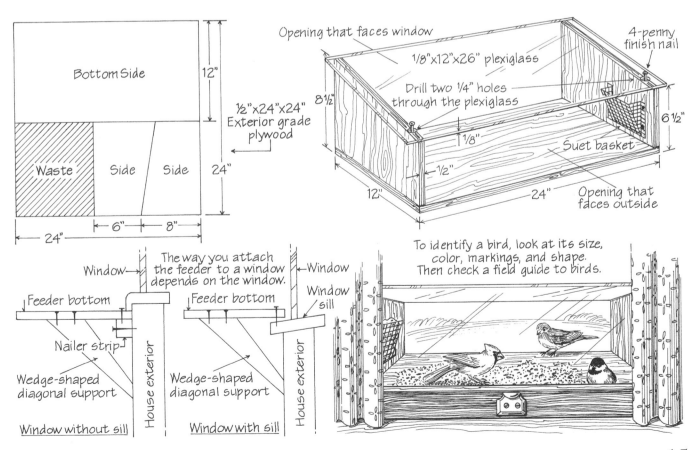

15

Winter EcoJournal

_____

_____

_____

_____

_____

_____

_____

_____

_____

_____

_____

_____

_____

_____

_____

December 14: Today the blizzard is over. The sky is a pale, watery blue. The limbs of the evergreens are bowed down with burdens of heavy snow. Long, glistening icicles hang from our roof. The ice and snow sparkle in the soft sunshine. It's *very* inviting, the kind of day when children tumble into the snow to slip and slide and sled.

The birds and squirrels have dug holes in the snow to get the birdseed that was scattered from the bird feeder yesterday. The birds have been recklessly darting up and down from a tree perch to the birdseed and then to another tree. Just when I was admiring a party of juncos—thinking how much they looked like two-colored Easter eggs with dark tops and white bottoms—one of the little juncos hit the window with a painful thud. It fell into the snow and lay still. I ran outside and gently scooped it up in my hands. The little bird was still breathing, so I brought it into the house and put it on a towel in a small cardboard box. I closed the box, leaving the bird in warm darkness.

I peeked in the box about every ten minutes. The junco was unconscious for quite a while, but gradually it got back on its feet and finally opened its eyes. I kept the bird in the box for another half hour to give it time to warm up and fully recover from the awful THUD. Then I took the box outside. As soon as I opened it, the junco flew low into the woods. I'm glad that little Easter egg didn't crack its shell!

Making Gifts for Nature Lovers

Nature lovers like to receive gifts made of natural materials, gifts that help them enjoy nature, or gifts that benefit the environment. Some of my favorite nature gifts can be easily made by kids: a nature wreath that will last until spring (*see page 11*), a pretty jar of winter potpourri (*page 13*), an edible pinecone (*page 19*), and woodpecker pizza or bird biscuits to feed winter birds (*page 23*).

One of the most welcome gifts in mid-winter is a container of flowers! It's easy to get flowers to bloom in winter if you start early enough. In mid-November, buy some paper-white narcissus bulbs at a garden center. They are tiny bulbs that produce white flowers that look like little daffodils. You can force them to bloom in four to six weeks—in time for Christmas. Choose little pots or jars, even baby food jars for individual blooms, and partly fill the jars with small pebbles. Gently push the bottoms of the bulbs into the pebbles until the bulbs stay upright. Then add water until it covers the bases of the bulbs. Keep the bulbs in a cool, dark place for about two weeks. Don't let the water level drop below the bulbs. After two weeks, place the bulbs in a cool, sunny spot and watch them grow. When they bloom, tie a ribbon around each jar and give them away. (Keep one for yourself!)

Another gift that is fun to make in winter is a snow candle. You will need one pound of wax from the supermarket, a half-gallon milk carton, enough crushed ice to fill the carton, a one-pound coffee can, and a length of cotton string for the wick. An adult should be present during the entire candle-making process. Cut the top off of the milk carton. Use a nail to poke a hole in the center of the bottom of the carton. Tie a knot in a length of string, thread it through the hole in the carton, and pull it up inside the carton to the top. To keep the string (the candle wick) straight, lay a pencil across the top of the carton and tie the string to the pencil. To melt the wax, bring an inch or two of water to a boil in a saucepan. Bend one side of a coffee can to form a pour spout, and put all of the wax in the can. Carefully place the can in the pan of boiling water until the wax melts. (*Never place the can of wax directly on the source of heat, because wax can explode at high temperatures*.) Fill the milk carton with crushed ice without disturbing the wick. Then have an adult pour the wax over the ice in the carton. When the wax cools and hardens, cut the knot off the wick at the bottom of the carton and cut the other end of the wick about ½ inch above the top of the candle. Use a knife to remove the carton from the candle. Work over a sink, because water from the melted ice will spill out. You will be surprised at the texture of your snow candle. What a beautiful gift!

What could be better than flowers in winter?

Never put a can of wax directly on a burner or flame.

Coffee can

Pour spout

Pencil

String (wick)

Milk carton

Sauce pan of boiling water

TO: Mom FROM: Lisa

A snow candle makes a beautiful gift!

Winter EcoJournal

_____
_____
_____
_____
_____
_____
_____
_____
_____
_____
_____
_____
_____
_____

December 18: I was walking on a quiet country road at dusk. The snowplow had piled shoulders of snow along both sides of the road. It was narrow and a little slippery, so I was concentrating more on my feet than on the winter scenery around me. But gradually I had the feeling that someone was watching me. It was silent in the gray dusk except for my own footsteps. Nothing moved around me, and yet I could sense someone staring at me with close attention. I peered into the whitish air, finally looking up into the tall trees. A great horned owl, looking like a dignified old gentleman two feet tall, looked me straight in the eye. The owl looked so serious that it made me laugh out loud. Even at the sound of my voice, the owl wasn't disturbed. It continued to watch me as I walked by, turning its head almost all the way around to stare over its back.

When Abercrombie was a little puppy not much bigger than a kitten, I would take him outside in the dark before we went to bed. On those cold winter nights, we would hear the haunting call of the great horned owl—and it often sounded dangerously near. I kept my eyes on the puppy as he poked around in and out of nighttime shadows. I didn't want the owl to swoop down and catch Abercrombie in its talons!

18

Make a Pinecone You Can Eat

When a squirrel chews on a pinecone, you know it must be delicious! They nibble and gnaw until there is nothing left but a slim pencil of woody core. You can find the knobby "pencils" under a squirrel's favorite perch. Birds, rabbits, chipmunks, and bears eat the tasty, oily seeds of pinecones.

If you would like to eat a pinecone that is more suitable for people, you can make one. All you need are eight ounces of cream cheese, half a stick of margarine, and two six-ounce cans of smoked almonds. Let the cream cheese and margarine stand at room temperature until they are soft. Then use a spoon or mixer to stir them together in a bowl.

After carefully washing your hands, shape the cream cheese/margarine mixture into a fat cone (you might say, *pinecone*) shape. Beginning at the bottom of the cone, push the smaller, pointed end of an almond part way into the cream cheese mixture. Push an entire row of almonds into the cream cheese all the way around the base of the cone. Then form a second row above the first, making sure that each almond in the second row is placed above and between two almonds in the first row. Continue forming rows of almonds until the entire cone is covered with almonds. Then gently cup your hands around the cone to force the almonds upward, so that they look exactly like the scales on a pinecone. Serve the cream cheese pinecone on a plate decorated with a real pinecone and a sprig of evergreen. Eat the pinecone with party crackers. Hmmm!

You can do an interesting experiment with a ripe, brown pinecone. On a dry day, choose a pinecone that is "open." (The scales are not closed tightly against the core of the cone.) Sprinkle the pinecone generously with water. In about an hour, the cone will be shut. Let it dry and the cone will open again. Pinecones close up in wet weather to protect their seeds from getting wet and falling straight down. If the seedlings grew directly under the parent tree, they wouldn't have enough room, sunshine, or water to grow well. In dry weather, pinecones open up, so that their winged seeds can fly to a better location. The cones continue to open and shut with the weather even when they no longer have seeds in them.

To make a tasty pinecone, all you need are cream cheese, margarine, and almonds.

Look carefully at this illustration to see how to arrange the rows of almonds.

SMOKED ALMONDS

CREAM CHEESE

Try this experiment with an open brown pinecone: Wet the pinecone and watch the scales shut. When the pinecone dries, the scales will open again!

Winter EcoJournal

_____

_____

_____

_____

_____

_____

_____

_____

_____

December 22: Our family likes to decorate a living tree for Christmas. We can only keep it inside for about a week, so we bring it in close to Christmas—today! We had already chosen the tree we wanted from Bob's evergreen nursery, where he plants Norway spruce seedlings every year. Even the tallest evergreens, the ones planted fifteen years ago, look small outside. They are dwarfed by the tall oaks, maples, and sycamores in the woods around them. But when we stood next to the tree we had chosen, it looked *plenty* big. It's ten feet tall and beautifully shaped. I was delighted to find an abandoned bird nest in it. The nest can be one of the decorations!

Bob "root pruned" the tree last year by digging a circle around it, cutting the long roots and forcing new roots to grow close to the tree. But even so, it was hard work for Bob and our son-in-law Jim to dig the tree and to lift the heavy root ball onto a large square of burlap. They tied the burlap around the tree trunk. Then they lifted the tree onto the front-end loader of the tractor and brought it to the house. We all worked to set the tree upright in a big metal tub and drag it into the living room. Thank goodness we have a high ceiling!

Our daughter Sandi watered the tree and covered the tub with a pretty Christmas cloth. We wrapped strings of tiny lights from branch to branch. They look like faraway stars. We hung dried apple and orange slices and cinnamon sticks on the tree with narrow red ribbon. Then we decorated it with bunches of dried flowers and bittersweet vines. We accidentally scattered red and yellow bittersweet berries all over the room. Bailey helped by batting them under the furniture. Charlie, who never causes trouble, slept behind the tree in a "secret place." We invited the men to come see our Christmas tree and spent a long time admiring it.

20

A Living Tradition

An old tradition, which dates back to the sixteenth century in northern Europe, is alive and popular today. In fact, it brings life to a dull winter landscape. What is this new-old tradition? It is decorating a Christmas tree for the birds. Even if you don't celebrate Christmas, you can trim a tree that will attract wildlife to your yard. The tree itself will be bright and beautiful, but just wait until the birds find it! Round red cardinals and lively blue jays will become living decorations.

Use your imagination to create edible ornaments for your tree. Think of food that is good for birds, and then string them into garlands, or think of ways to hang them from the boughs or limbs of the tree. Here are some suggestions:

- String garlands of popcorn, peanuts in shells, cranberries, raisins, dates, or orange peel.

- Hang pinecones or bagels, which have been spread with peanut butter and then dipped in birdseed and a little sand. (Birds need *grit*, or sand, in their diet, but it is hard to find on frozen ground.)

- Use a hollowed-out orange or grapefruit rind as a container for nuts, stale bread, apple wedges, raisins, and suet chunks.

- Tie small bunches of wheat together and hang them.

- Fill plastic net onion bags with chunks of suet. Mix in some sand.

- Hang apples, carrots, donuts, bagels, or colored Indian corn with ribbon.

Garland of popcorn, peanuts, cranberries, raisins, dates, and orange peel

Create a new tradition: Decorate a snowman for the birds.

Suet in onion bag

Indian corn

Pinecones and bagels, spread with peanut butter, dipped in birdseed

Carrot

Wheat

Apple

Donut

Chains of peanuts and orange peel

Grapefruit rind filled with nuts, fruit, bread, and suet

Carrot

Prunes

Apple half

Raisins

Pinecones with peanut butter and birdseed

Water for birds

You can decorate any tree for birds, but an evergreen gives cover, too.

Winter EcoJournal

_____

_____

_____

_____

_____

_____

_____

_____

_____

_____

December 25: Our Christmas Day was crisp and cold outside, but warm with love and happiness inside. Our house bulged with three generations of family. We opened gifts and laughed at surprises, played music and sang songs, told jokes and family stories, prayed and played and cooked and ate too much and napped and ate again. Every room was filled with fragrance: the sweet-and-spicy, outdoor smell of our Christmas tree with its cinnamon sticks and bittersweet berries; the irresistible smell of pies and fresh bread baking in the oven; and another fragrance—not really a smell at all—of memories and dreams that bind a family together.

We had gifts for all the animals. Abercrombie got a new sweater. Charlie got a cozy cat bed. Bailey got his own toilet brush. (Bailey works the bathroom cabinet open to chew on the toilet brush, so I thought I'd buy him a clean one!) Abercrombie didn't like his sweater and worked his way out of it. Charlie didn't want to sleep in his new bed. He settled in his place behind the Christmas tree. Bailey *loved* his toilet brush. He chewed on it, balled up on it and kicked it, guarded it, and finally fell asleep with his chin on it.

After dinner, we took an apple block out to the deer feeder. It's a large block of compressed grain, molasses, salt, and apple, which I bought at the feed mill. We tied the fat rind from our Christmas ham to a branch near the bird feeder. The insect-eating birds will pick it clean. And of course, the compost pile is laden with holiday leftovers. As I looked up at the dark sky, I felt Christmas overflowing into the night and all the way up to the stars.

22

Woodpecker Pizza and Bird Biscuits

The birds that keep us company all winter are like special gifts. Have you ever wanted to give something back to the birds that brighten winter? Something delicious? Like bacon grease and sand? Or cornmeal and sunflower seeds?

Many bird watchers have created treats for birds. (Bird treats can also be given as gifts to anyone who loves birds.) Start with the recipes given below. Then make up your own recipe with ingredients that birds like: fruit, nuts, seeds, corn, cornmeal, suet, bacon grease, peanut butter, and rolled oats. Don't forget to add a little sand. Most birds need grit in their diet to help them grind up their food and to give them minerals that they need. Besides sand, you can give birds wood ashes or canary grit from a pet store.

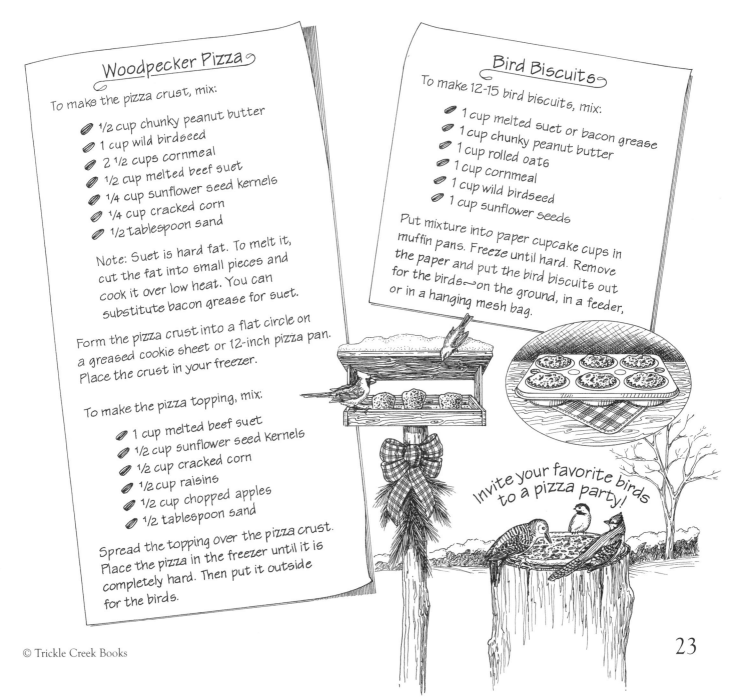

Woodpecker Pizza

To make the pizza crust, mix:

- ½ cup chunky peanut butter
- 1 cup wild birdseed
- 2 ½ cups cornmeal
- ½ cup melted beef suet
- ¼ cup sunflower seed kernels
- ¼ cup cracked corn
- ½ tablespoon sand

Note: Suet is hard fat. To melt it, cut the fat into small pieces and cook it over low heat. You can substitute bacon grease for suet.

Form the pizza crust into a flat circle on a greased cookie sheet or 12-inch pizza pan. Place the crust in your freezer.

To make the pizza topping, mix:

- 1 cup melted beef suet
- ½ cup sunflower seed kernels
- ½ cup cracked corn
- ½ cup raisins
- ½ cup chopped apples
- ½ tablespoon sand

Spread the topping over the pizza crust. Place the pizza in the freezer until it is completely hard. Then put it outside for the birds.

Bird Biscuits

To make 12-15 bird biscuits, mix:

- 1 cup melted suet or bacon grease
- 1 cup chunky peanut butter
- 1 cup rolled oats
- 1 cup cornmeal
- 1 cup wild birdseed
- 1 cup sunflower seeds

Put mixture into paper cupcake cups in muffin pans. Freeze until hard. Remove the paper and put the bird biscuits out for the birds—on the ground, in a feeder, or in a hanging mesh bag.

Invite your favorite birds to a pizza party!

Winter EcoJournal

_____
_____
_____
_____
_____
_____
_____
_____
_____
_____
_____
_____
_____
_____

December 28: This was an "icebox day," only 11 degrees. Bailey asked several times to go outside, but when I opened the door, he ducked his head and flattened his ears and backed away from the frigid cold. The rest of us didn't even consider going out.

The birds have been active all day—even at noontime, when they usually rest. I think they're working hard to keep warm. I'm so glad some of the birds stay with us through the coldest part of winter. It would be dull and lonely without them. I love the feisty little chickadees with their black caps, and the blue-gray nuthatches, which come down a tree headfirst. And the mourning doves with their haunting calls. And the checkered woodpeckers with red-splashed heads. And the serious little titmice and the warm brown Carolina wrens and the gorgeous blue jays and the beautiful pairs of cardinals. They brighten the cold, still, black-and-white landscape like flowers in a desert.

24

Project FeederWatch

It's so much fun to feed birds during the winter. We feel good about helping to care for wild birds when their natural food is scarce. And we enjoy their bright colors and eager flying and fluttering when they come to our bird feeders. But did you know that while you're watching birds for fun, you can also do authentic research that will help scientists study backyard birds?

Project FeederWatch invites you to watch birds once every two weeks from November through March. You are asked to count the kinds and numbers of birds at your feeder and to send the results to the Cornell Lab of Ornithology. (*Ornithology* is the science that studies birds.) Your findings can help scientists tell how certain bird populations are growing or declining and how they are distributed throughout our continent. FeederWatch results are published in science journals and popular magazines.

The regular fee to participate in Project FeederWatch is $15.00. When you join the project, you will receive a research kit with instructions, a color poster of common feeder birds, access to the FeederWatch web site (www.birds.cornell.edu/pfw/), and the newsletter, *Birdscope*.

Cardinal

Tufted Titmouse

To sign up for Project FeederWatch, call 1-800-843-BIRD or write to:

Project FeederWatch
Cornell Lab of Ornithology
P.O. Box 11
Ithaca, NY 14851-0011

Flicker

White-throated Sparrow

Junco

Project FeederWatch is sponsored by the Cornell Lab of Ornithology, the National Audubon Society, Bird Studies Canada, and the Canadian Nature Federation.

Winter EcoJournal

_____

_____

_____

_____

_____

_____

_____

_____

_____

_____

_____

_____

_____

January 1: The first day of the year offers a new beginning. It's a good time to think about the way our world is and about the way we would like it to be. I know what I want. I want to breathe pure air and drink fresh water. I want to have healthy forests, and meadows of wildflowers, and rich wetlands. I want ponds full of frogs, and rivers filled with fish, and oceans brimming with strange underwater creatures. I want yellow butterflies in my garden and bluebirds in the orchard. Don't you?

So far we haven't been very good stewards of our Earth. Too many people have acted out of greed or carelessness or ignorance. I pray that in the new year, we might see what we are doing to our environment and to life on Earth—and resolve to act more wisely and kindly.

As a nature writer and a teacher, my work is to teach kids to care for the Earth. When children learn to observe nature more and more closely, they naturally love our environment and want to protect it. I believe today's children are more "eco-smart" than any generation before them. I think they'll be better guardians of the Earth than other generations have been—because they *must* be! The welfare of our world depends on it.

Plans for a Green New Year

When people talk about a product or a plan that is "green," they are often referring to something that is friendly to our environment. Anything that helps keep our planet clean and green is worth doing. Have you thought about how you can help? You might want to make some New Year resolutions to help care for our Earth. Some examples are:

- I will sort the trash to separate materials that can be recycled.
- I will wet my toothbrush and then turn the water off while I brush my teeth.
- I will carry a fabric tote bag when I shop, so that I don't have to use a plastic bag or a paper bag.
- I will make a compost pile, so that my family can use compost as a natural fertilizer and mulch. Then we won't have to use chemicals, and we won't add our yard wastes to landfills. (*See "Make the Most of Compost" on page 25 of* A Kid's Fall EcoJournal.)
- I will use both sides of a sheet of paper.
- I will plant a tree.
- I will build a backyard wildlife refuge. (*See "Save a Place for Wildlife" on page 9 of* A Kid's Spring EcoJournal.)
- I will not litter even if I have to carry trash until I find a waste bin.
- I will turn the light off when I leave a room.
- I will plant a butterfly garden.
- I will build a birdhouse.
- I will build a small pond for wildlife. (*See "Make an Eco-Pond" on page 43 of* A Kid's Spring EcoJournal.)

You could post your resolutions on an "Eco-Calendar." Glue a calendar for each month on a piece of poster paper or colored paper. Above each calendar, draw a nature picture that is appropriate for the month. (Or take a nature photo each month.) Add your resolution in large letters to remind yourself—and your family—to be "eco-smart"!

Winter EcoJournal

January 3: The weather has been frigid for days. The highest temperature today was 20 degrees and the wind was painfully cold. The cats and Abercrombie were restless. They wanted to go outside, but they certainly didn't want to stay there. Both cats have winter fur as tight and thick as a plush carpet. They have warm fur between and around the pads on their feet. Before he goes outside, Bailey shakes each leg and fluffs up his fur. I can almost see him putting on a snowsuit. Bailey (my white snow-cat) can stay outside for an hour or more, but Charlie and Abercrombie come back in after only a few minutes. Charlie is beautiful with a dusting of snow on his back.

I was restless, too. I made up my mind to take a walk no matter how cold it was. As I slogged through the snow to the pond, the cold made the bones of my face ache. The pond was frozen smooth except where bedraggled cattails poked through the ice. Trickle Creek was trickling. The edges of the creek were icy, and there were wonderful, splashy icicles on some of the rocks. It was pretty, but I didn't stay long. I decided that I wanted to be cooped up in the house again—fast! I think I'm a Charlie, not a Bailey.

The Deep Sleep of Hibernation

In winter, many animals have trouble finding food—just when they need more food than usual to produce enough energy to keep them warm. For some animals, the solution to this urgent problem is to *hibernate*. A hibernating animal falls into a deep, almost death-like sleep. Its body temperature falls, so that it is almost as cold as the surrounding air. Its breathing and heart rate slow down and become very faint. The animal slowly converts stored fat into energy. (Animals that hibernate eat extra food during late summer and early fall to fatten themselves up!)

True hibernators are warm-blooded animals, mostly mammals—such as bats, groundhogs, and hamsters—and a few birds. Their body temperature drops well below normal. Bears sleep during the winter, but their body temperature stays near normal, so many scientists don't consider them to be true hibernators. All amphibians and reptiles, such as turtles, frogs, and snakes, sleep through the winter. But they are not true hibernators, because they are cold-blooded and their temperature is always the same as their surroundings, even when they are awake. Many insects enter a kind of hibernation.

True hibernators don't sleep soundly all winter. They take a series of naps, and they seem to be able to wake up when they want to. If the weather gets too cold, hibernating animals may wake up and burrow deeper or move to a warmer place. They become active again when warm spring days bring them out of hibernation. Cold-blooded animals sleep through the winter. They can only be roused from hibernation when their bodies warm up as the weather becomes milder.

If you have room in your yard or if your school has a nature trail, one of the best kinds of shelter you can provide for wildlife at *any* season is a brush pile. Make a large pile of logs, tree limbs, and shrubbery branches. (After Christmas, lay your Christmas tree on the ground on its side. It makes a great base for a brush pile.) When it snows, look for tracks around the brush pile to tell you which animals are finding shelter there. For example, you may see tracks of animals that don't hibernate, such as rabbits, opossums, skunks, or birds.

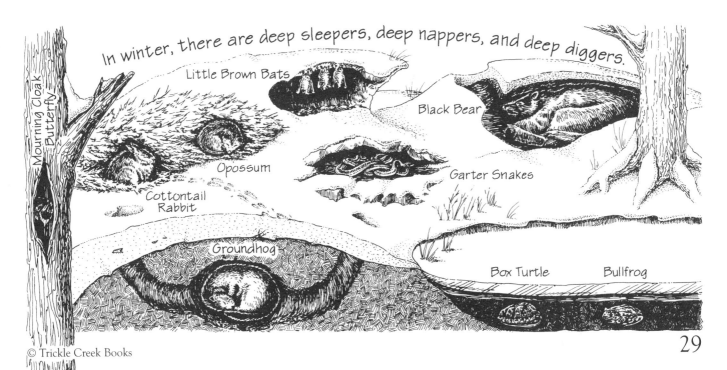

In winter, there are deep sleepers, deep nappers, and deep diggers.

Mourning Cloak Butterfly · Little Brown Bats · Black Bear · Opossum · Garter Snakes · Cottontail Rabbit · Groundhog · Box Turtle · Bullfrog

Winter EcoJournal

_____

_____

_____

_____

_____

_____

_____

_____

_____

_____

_____

_____

_____

January 6: Bob and I took our lunch to the Yellow Breeches Creek for a "car picnic." It was a car picnic because it was too cold to eat outside the car. We parked near the water and watched the ducks while we ate. The Yellow Breeches is a wide trout stream with clear water gurgling under and around sheets of greenish ice. Two handsome mallard ducks with green-satin heads bobbed in the icy water as if it were a warm bath. The female mallards, a mottled brown like the oak leaves still hanging on a winter tree, were diving for food, tilting straight down with their tails in the air.

After awhile, the ducks worked their way downstream, leaving one lone female behind. She stood perfectly still on an island of ice. She never moved while we finished our lunch. She didn't move when we got out of the car. She didn't budge when we called to her. It occurred to me that her feet might be frozen to the ice! How awful! We threw some snowballs into the rushing water on both sides of her island perch. She crouched down, but she didn't move.

I was convinced that she was frozen fast to the ice. I started thinking of things that Bob could do to rescue her. Most of them involved wading into the freezing creek. (He could wear rubber waders.) He didn't seem to _want_ to rescue her. While we were arguing about it, she calmly flew away.

30

Snow Experiments

When the temperature of the air between the clouds and the ground is at or below 32 degrees, water vapor in the air freezes and crystallizes. The flat, six-sided crystals that form are snowflakes. Snowflakes occur in an infinite variety of shapes. No one has ever found two identical snowflakes!

The next time it snows in your area, see if you can guess the temperature by observing the snowflakes as they fall. If the snowflakes are large and wet—if they look like falling popcorn—the temperature is probably near the freezing point of water (32 degrees). If the snow is like fine sugar, glittering and dry, the temperature is probably much colder. After you watch the snowflakes fall, check an outdoor thermometer to see how well you guessed the temperature.

To look at snowflakes more closely, take a piece of black construction paper outside and catch some snowflakes as they fall. Try to look at them with a magnifying lens before they melt! Can you see their six sides?

It's interesting to see how much (or how little) water is produced when snow melts. Fill a measuring cup with snow. Use a ruler to measure how many inches of snow are in the cup. Then let the snow melt. Does one cup of snow produce one cup of water? Measure the water in inches. It usually takes ten inches of dry snow to make one inch of water. If the weather is extremely cold and the snow is light and powdery, it may take thirty inches of snow to make one inch of water! Can you find out how much snow it takes to produce a cup of water on a very cold day and also on a warmer day?

Do an experiment to see which melts faster—clean snow or dirty snow. Collect two samples of clean snow in two identical containers. Sprinkle one sample of snow with dark ashes or coal dust. Set the two containers of snow side by side in a sunny place. Which one melts first? Clean, white snow relects light and heat from the sun. (Freshly fallen snow reflects about 95 percent of the sun's heat back into space.) Dirty snow—dark snow—*absorbs* light and heat.

Snowflakes are tiny, icy crystals with perfect six-sided shapes.

Snow   Melted Snow

Which snow will melt first, clean snow or dirty snow?

Winter EcoJournal

_____

_____

_____

_____

_____

_____

_____

_____

_____

January 7: Last night, I opened the door to let Abercrombie go out, not realizing that an opossum was at the other side of the door. There was an alarmed confusion of hissing and yelping. Abercrombie growled his loudest growl, dove forward, then leaped backward. His hackles rose. A brown ruff of hair stood straight up along his neck and back. The opossum was backed into a corner. Its beady black eyes shone like polished coal. Its long, drooling mouth was open in what looked like a wide grin, revealing its teeth—all fifty of them! (An opossum has more teeth than any other mammal in North America.) No wonder Abercrombie's hackles were up!

Abercrombie is not a hunter. As far as I know, he's never hurt another animal. This was a distressing situation for a dog who is not used to fighting. His barking grew more and more shrill and excited. Suddenly the opossum fell over on its side and lay motionless, its eyes and mouth still open.

"What happened?" I asked, as we pulled Abercrombie back into the house.

"The possum is playing possum," Bob answered. We went outside to look more closely. We looked at its shaggy hair and rat-like tail. We looked at its teeth. Bob gently rattled a stick between the animal's upper and lower teeth—not to hurt it or frighten it, but to test this business of "playing possum." The opossum didn't flinch or bite down or even blink. Apparently, it was in a kind of stupor that made it appear to be dead. It's an old, old method of protection for opossums.

About ten minutes later, the opossum woke up and slowly waddled off into the woods.

32

Ice Experiments

On one of those "deep freeze" days of winter, look for ice outside. Examine icicles hanging from a roof, ice formations at the edge of a rushing creek, icy puddles, ice-coated branches after an ice storm, or thick ice on a pond. (*NEVER walk, skate, or play on ice-covered water unless an adult is with you and has declared it to be safe*.) Break the ice on a small puddle with your boots or a sturdy stick. How thick is the ice?

Water is a strange substance, because it increases in volume—it gets bigger in size—when it freezes. As water changes to ice, the water molecules fit together in a certain pattern and take up more room than they did as molecules of liquid water. You can easily demonstrate this odd property of water. Simply fill a plastic container to the very brim with water and place it in a freezer overnight. What does it look like in the morning? Can you tell that water increases in volume when it freezes?

Because the molecules in ice aren't packed together as closely as they are in liquid water, ice is less dense than water. That's why ice will float in water. Try floating an ice cube in a glass of water. How much of the ice is below the water level? Now do you see why icebergs in the ocean are so dangerous to ships? Most of the iceberg is below the water line.

Have a contest with a couple of friends to see who can melt an ice cube first. Gather some materials that might be helpful: several straws, some salt, aluminum foil, black construction paper, a sheet of plastic foam packing, and a wooden spoon for applying pressure to the ice cube. The rules of the competition are that you can touch the ice cube but you can't crush it, and you can use any of the gathered materials to help make the ice cube melt. Give each person an ice cube. Ready, set, melt!

After you have competed to find out how to melt an ice cube, try another contest with the same materials to see how to *keep* an ice cube from melting. This time, the person whose ice cube lasts the longest is the winner.

It's easy to prove that water increases in volume when it freezes.

Can you think of other materials that would make an ice cube melt or keep it from melting?

Wooden spoon

Foam packing

Straw

SALT

Black paper

Foil

Winter EcoJournal

_____

_____

_____

_____

_____

_____

_____

_____

_____

_____

January 12: It snowed last night, and this morning there were fresh, clear tracks everywhere. I bundled up and went outside, determined to investigate them. I didn't want Abercrombie or the cats to go with me, because they would probably disturb the perfect tracks. But it wasn't easy getting out the door without them. As I pushed Charlie back inside with my hand against his nose, Bailey leaped over him and ran behind an evergreen shrub. I pulled him out and stuffed him back in the house.

Well, at least I could identify the first tracks I looked at. They were Bailey's long leaps. Interesting! Then I looked under the bird feeder. The *hoppers*, birds that spend most of their time in trees, left prints with their feet side by side. The *walkers*, birds that feed mostly on the ground, left "walking" prints almost like a person's. There were squirrel prints under the feeder, too, and holes in the snow where squirrels had dug down to find scattered corn.

I was able to follow a set of deer prints, which came out of the woods to the deer feeder and then continued right up to the shrubs in my flower beds. The deer have eaten the azalea bushes down to woody stubs and cropped the buds and leaves from the rhododendrons. I know they're hungry, but do they have to eat my flowers? I followed the deer prints all the way to Bob's evergreen nursery. Oh, no! The deer have been eating the little Christmas trees. I could see where several deer had bedded down. The snow was packed down in a circular hollow. In places, the snow had melted where the deer lie down together, and green grass was visible. How nice to sleep near the tender little evergreen trees—little midnight snacks!

34

Tracking Animals in Snow

Winter is a hard time for animals. Cold-blooded animals, such as frogs, turtles, and snakes, sleep through the cold months. Some warm-blooded animals, such as groundhogs and bats, hibernate. Many birds, such as robins and wild geese, *migrate*, or move to a place with a different climate. Still, a surprising number of birds and mammals stay put and go about their daily business as usual. They walk or run, rest, eat, hunt, flee, and play. If there is snow on the ground, you can look for signs of animal activity. With careful observation—and a lively imagination—you may be able to read amazing stories in the snow.

Animal tracks that are found in mud are usually identified by observing the number of toes and claw marks on a footprint. (*See "A Track Trap" on page 47 of* A Kid's Spring EcoJournal.) But tracks found in soft or deep snow may not show any details, and tracks in melting snow may be twice their normal size. You may only see holes in the snow and "drag marks" where a small animal's belly brushed the snow or a deer dragged its feet as it walked or a bird took flight, leaving wing-marks. Instead of looking closely at footprints, practice looking at the track pattern on the trail left by an animal. Look for track patterns that have alternating prints, two prints, or four prints. (Check the illustration below.)

It's fun to follow animal tracks in snow. As you go, look for signs that will help you identify the animal that made the trail. For example, cottontail rabbits leave round pellets (their droppings) at feeding and resting places. They also neatly clip off buds and twigs about a foot from the ground. Squirrels sometimes build large leaf nests high in trees. You may find discarded pinecone scales and cores, nutshells, or cherry seeds in a tree cavity. Foxes hunt small rodents by digging in the snow. If they catch their prey, you may find signs of blood or fur. Skunks often leave evidence of digging and, of course, an unmistakable scent. (You know!) Deer make oval-shaped beds in the snow, where you might find deer hair.

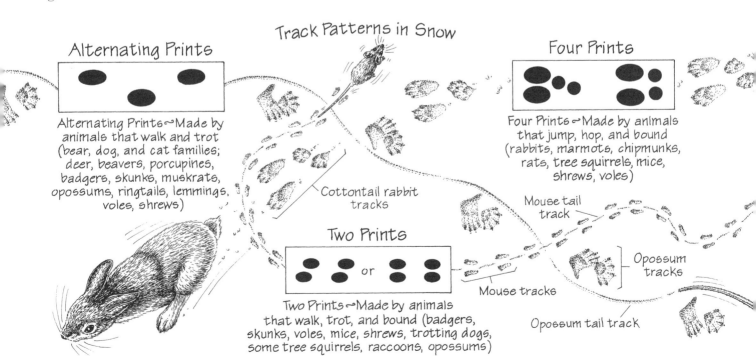

Track Patterns in Snow

Alternating Prints

Alternating Prints~Made by animals that walk and trot (bear, dog, and cat families; deer, beavers, porcupines, badgers, skunks, muskrats, opossums, ringtails, lemmings, voles, shrews)

Cottontail rabbit tracks

Two Prints

Two Prints~Made by animals that walk, trot, and bound (badgers, skunks, voles, mice, shrews, trotting dogs, some tree squirrels, raccoons, opossums)

Four Prints

Four Prints~Made by animals that jump, hop, and bound (rabbits, marmots, chipmunks, rats, tree squirrels, mice, shrews, voles)

Mouse tail track

Mouse tracks

Opossum tracks

Opossum tail track

Winter EcoJournal

January 17: The temperature climbed to 50 degrees today. I took a long walk through a landscape muffled in fog. Oh, these gray, gray days! We've only seen a few glimpses of sun since November. As I walked, a cold breath of gray mist settled on my face. Trees loomed up out of the fog like faded newspaper photos with softened lines and blurred colors. There was no sound to be heard. My own footsteps sounded far away—as if I were following myself. I stopped at the pond and looked at smudgy reflections drawn in smoke. When I came out of the woods, the fog lay faintly green on a wide meadow. The hills beyond the meadow were blotted out, *fogged* out.

For me, January and February are long. It's not so much the cold that bothers me as the grayness. Suddenly, I had a great idea! I drove to a large country market and walked up and down the aisles between tables laden with flowering plants. I drank in color and fragrance and light. I admired giant ferns with glossy leaves, exotic cacti with outrageous flowers, lilies and African violets and miniature roses. My eyes danced from color to color—lemon yellow, magenta, brilliant orange, deep pink. I left feeling energized and happy. (I don't want to admit how many flowers I bought.)

Acid Snow and Cabbage Water

A fresh snowfall makes all the world look clean and bright. But is snow *really* clean? If our water and air are not pure, then our snow will not be pure either. You can do a simple test to find out if your snow is polluted. Collect about ten cups of snow and let it melt. Cover the mouth of a measuring cup or other container with a paper towel. Pour the melted snow through the paper towel into the container. Carefully examine the paper towel for tiny, dirty particles. Look at the particles through a magnifying lens, too. How clean was the snow you collected? Collect a second sample of snow beside a road. (Watch for traffic!) Test the snow for pollution. Was it dirtier than the first sample? What does this tell us about the purity of our air and about pollution from vehicles?

Another pollution problem is invisible but very serious. Certain industrial activities, like burning coal to generate electricity, pollute the air and cause acid rain in summer—or acid snow in winter. When coal is burned, *sulfur dioxide* is released into the air. The sulfur dioxide slowly reacts with oxygen and moisture in the air to form *sulfuric acid*. When coal, oil, or natural gas are burned, *nitric oxides* are released. The nitric oxides react with oxygen and moisture in the air to form *nitric acid*. When these acids are brought to the ground in rain or snow, they can harm plants and animals. In spring, acid-laden snow melts and runs into streams and lakes, polluting the water. Sometimes the chemistry of the water is so changed that fish, amphibians, and aquatic plants die.

An interesting way to test for acid in your snow is to use cabbage water! Fill a jar with small pieces of red cabbage leaves. Ask an adult to heat *distilled* water until it boils and to pour the boiling water over the cabbage leaves. When the cabbage water cools, pour it through a strainer into a second container. Throw the cabbage leaves away. Mix a sample of melted snow with some of the blue cabbage water. If the cabbage water turns red, there is acid in the snow. If you want to do a more precise test, you can buy litmus paper at a science store or school supply store. (See the illustration below.)

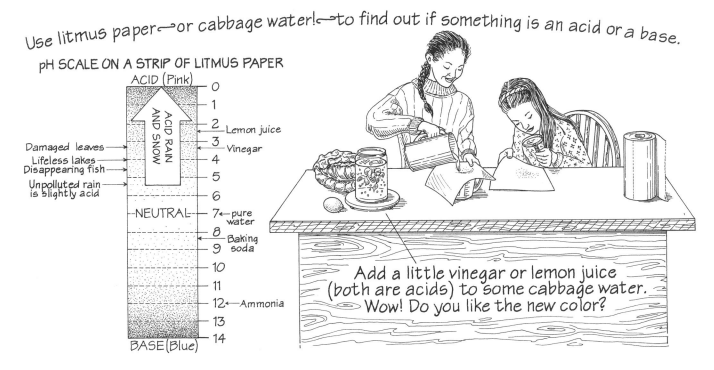

Use litmus paper↪or cabbage water!↪to find out if something is an acid or a base.

pH SCALE ON A STRIP OF LITMUS PAPER

ACID (Pink)

ACID RAIN AND SNOW

- 0
- 1
- 2 ← Lemon juice
- 3 ← Vinegar
- 4
- 5
- 6
- 7 ← pure water
- 8
- 9 ← Baking soda
- 10
- 11
- 12 ← Ammonia
- 13
- 14

Damaged leaves →
Lifeless lakes →
Disappearing fish →
Unpolluted rain is slightly acid →

NEUTRAL

BASE (Blue)

Add a little vinegar or lemon juice (both are acids) to some cabbage water. Wow! Do you like the new color?

Winter EcoJournal

_____

_____

_____

_____

_____

_____

_____

_____

_____

_____

_____

_____

_____

January 22: A week ago, the Susquehanna River was entirely covered with smooth ice. But after a few days of unusually warm weather, the ice is melting and moving. This morning as I drove across a long bridge that spans the river, I was dazzled by sunshine reflecting off mounds of crushed and broken ice. They sparkled like big heaps of diamonds. Patches of clear, green water flowed beneath the ice, urging it downstream.

Years ago on a frigid February night, Bob and I were eating at a favorite restaurant. In the summer, we like to eat on a long deck overlooking the river, but of course the deck area was closed in February. During our meal, we realized that something strange was going on. People were going out into the freezing night to stand on the deck. We were overcome with curiosity, left our dinners, found our coats, and went outside to look at the river.

No one spoke. We all listened to an enormous sound that filled the night. It was like the voice of a giant whispering, "Hush-sh-sh." It was the sound of thick ice breaking up and beginning to move slowly on the current of the river. As great chunks of ice collided with the pilings of the bridge, the ice rose up out of the water in slow motion, crunching and whispering and splashing down again like a great, ungainly whale. It was unforgettable.

Make Ice Cream in a Snow Freezer

When I was a child, we made snow ice cream by adding milk and eggs and sugar and vanilla to snow. It was a special treat that we could only have in winter. Today, children can't eat snow ice cream, because most snow is polluted in some way. But you can still make ice cream in a snow freezer!

Choose one of the recipes given below to make Snow-Frozen Vanilla Ice Cream or Snow-Frozen Strawberry Sherbet. Follow the directions for preparing the ice cream or sherbet mixture. Then pour the mixture into a plastic carton or bowl.

To make a snow freezer, fill a large bowl with snow or crushed ice. Add one cup of salt for every three cups of snow, and stir the salt and snow together. Place the plastic carton of ice cream mix in the large bowl of snow. Cover the bowl. The ice cream is ready to eat as soon as it freezes. You can check it after about fifteen minutes. If too much of the snow melts, add more snow and salt.

Note: Pure water freezes—and melts—at 32° F, or 0° C. Salt lowers the temperature at which water freezes and melts. In fact, the more salt that is added to water, the lower its freezing point becomes. Test this by putting two containers of water, one with salt and one without, in the freezer or outside on a freezing day. Which one freezes first? Can you see why salt spread on icy roads melts the ice? And why salt added to a snow freezer makes the snow colder—cold enough to freeze ice cream?

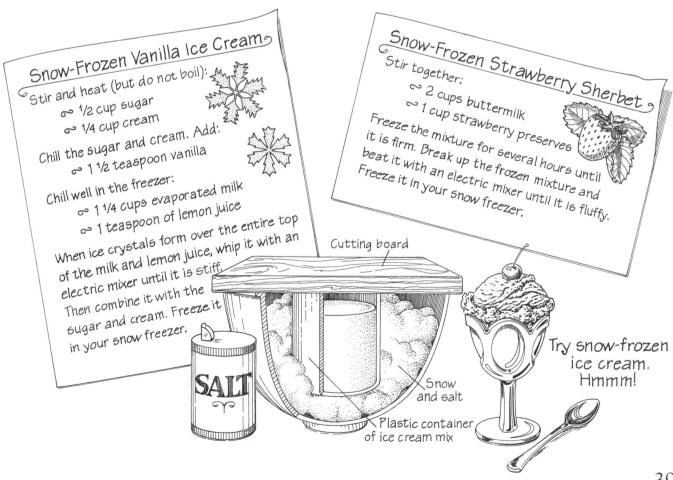

Snow-Frozen Vanilla Ice Cream

Stir and heat (but do not boil):
- ½ cup sugar
- ¼ cup cream

Chill the sugar and cream. Add:
- 1 ½ teaspoon vanilla

Chill well in the freezer:
- 1 ¼ cups evaporated milk
- 1 teaspoon of lemon juice

When ice crystals form over the entire top of the milk and lemon juice, whip it with an electric mixer until it is stiff. Then combine it with the sugar and cream. Freeze it in your snow freezer.

Snow-Frozen Strawberry Sherbet

Stir together:
- 2 cups buttermilk
- 1 cup strawberry preserves

Freeze the mixture for several hours until it is firm. Break up the frozen mixture and beat it with an electric mixer until it is fluffy. Freeze it in your snow freezer.

Cutting board

Snow and salt

SALT

Plastic container of ice cream mix

Try snow-frozen ice cream. Hmmm!

Winter EcoJournal

January 27: Today I walked beside Trickle Creek, enjoying the small sounds that a creek makes under ice. In the distance, crows were having a lively argument at the tops of their voices. Somewhere nearby, I could hear the echoing ring of a woodpecker drilling a hole in a tree to search for insects. I listened carefully. Each species of woodpecker has a particular rhythm of hammering with its beak. This one drummed louder and faster toward the middle, then faded off toward the end. I think my heart beat a little tattoo of its own. I was listening to the pileated woodpecker, the biggest, showiest, most-difficult-to-get-your-eyes-on woodpecker of all!

I quietly followed the drumming sound, and in just a few minutes, I spotted the woodpecker. It was working its way across a dead limb on an old oak, twisting its head and beak with every blow. Wood chips flew in all directions! I sat down on a cold log and watched the woodpecker work for five or ten minutes before it flew away. What a beautiful bird! It was more than a foot tall, and its brilliant red crest was a flame of color in the winter woods.

What Breaks the Winter Silence?

The next time you walk in the countryside or in a park on a winter day, be still. Don't make a sound. Listen to the quiet that spreads around you. What breaks the winter silence? You may hear the lonely call of a single bird, the secret trickle of melting snow, a rush of wind, or the crunch of your feet on frozen ground or icy snow.

Use a battery-operated tape recorder to make a recording of the winter sounds you hear. Record comments and explanations in your own words, too. For example, as the recorder picks up the cry of a bird, record yourself describing what the bird is doing: "A crow flew away when it saw me and that was its call." Later, when you listen to your recording, see if there were some sounds around you that you didn't hear at the time.

One of the sweetest, eeriest winter sounds is the haunting call of an owl at night. Sometimes one owl will answer another in a kind of two-part song. Sometimes—if you can imitate the owl's call—an owl will answer *you*! To make an owl caller, you will need a piece of white plastic drain pipe, 1½" in diameter and 6" long. (This pipe, which is used under sinks, can be found in the plumbing section of a building supply store.) The pipe should have a *flange*, a projecting rim, on one end. Drill a ⅜-inch hole in the pipe two inches from the end with the flange. Use epoxy glue (follow the directions on the container to mix the epoxy) to attach the lid from a spice jar to the flange end of the pipe. The flange is glued to the top of the lid. On the other end of the pipe, glue a rotary top, which has been removed from a container of crazy salt or lemon pepper. Rotate the top, so that the largest hole is completely open.

Cut a 2-inch length from the lid of a ballpoint pen. File or sand half of one end of the pen to form an angle at the end. (See the illustration below.) Hold the pen piece above the hole in the side of the pipe, and blow through the pen piece. Move the pen piece around until you find the position that produces the loudest, deepest sound. Mark the location and glue the pen piece exactly there, securing it with masking tape until the glue dries. Now you have an owl caller! To imitate a barred owl call, copy the rhythm of these sentences: "Who cooks for you? Who cooks for you all?" Then listen for an answer in the night.

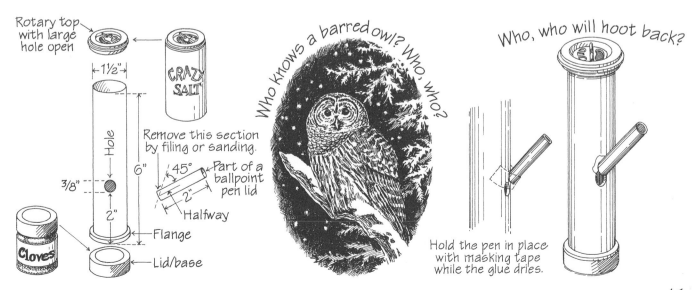

Rotary top with large hole open

1½"

CRAZY SALT

Hole

Remove this section by filing or sanding.

6"

45°

Part of a ballpoint pen lid

2"

Halfway

3/8"

2"

Cloves

Flange

Lid/base

Who knows a barred owl? Who, who?

Who, who will hoot back?

Hold the pen in place with masking tape while the glue dries.

Winter EcoJournal

_____

_____

_____

_____

_____

_____

_____

_____

_____

_____

_____

February 2: Today we met an animal that we had never seen before! Our friend Don trapped a little flying squirrel in the attic of his cabin. Since flying squirrels are only active at night and seldom come down from trees to the ground, most people have never seen one. Don brought the squirrel to us, so that we could look it over before releasing it at Trickle Creek.

What a beautiful little animal! Its fur was soft and silky, gray velvet on its back and white satin on its belly. It had a snub-nosed face, round ears, and big black eyes. (You can tell a *nocturnal* animal—an animal that is active at night—by its big, big eyes.) Its tail was furry but flat. Its body was about five inches long. The most interesting feature of the flying squirrel was a fold of loose, furred skin along its sides between the fore and hind legs. It looked exactly like a fur cape attached to its wrists and ankles. The cape, like a Superman cape, enables the squirrel to "fly." It doesn't really fly, but it can sail 120 feet after leaping into the air from a tall tree. Wouldn't that be fun to see?

We released the flying squirrel at dusk at the base of a hickory tree near the pond. Flying squirrels love hickory nuts, and the tree already had an unoccupied birdhouse on it. Maybe the squirrel will make the birdhouse its home. When we opened the carrier-cage, the squirrel spent just a moment looking around, leaped onto the trunk of the tree, and sprinted up into the highest branches. We'll probably never see the flying squirrel again, but I'm so glad we saw it once.

42

Winter Secrets

When trees have lost their sheltering leaves, you can discover some interesting secrets among their bare limbs. Look closely at a tree. Let your eyes roam over every branch. You might see an abandoned bird nest that held a family of little birds a few months ago. Or you might see a large leaf nest high in the tree. It is probably a squirrel nest with squirrels inside it. Squirrels prefer to live in tree cavities, but when they can't find a cavity to live in, they build a snug leaf nest. (*Cavities* are large or small holes in a tree.) Don't forget to look for cavities, especially in dead trees or in dead branches of a living tree. If you see a cavity that you can reach, look for signs that might tell you what kind of animal could have nested there—or is wintering there right now! Look for scratches made by an animal with claws. Or sawdust made by an animal that has chewed the tree to make a bigger entrance hole. Or nutshells and cherry seeds left by an animal that was eating or storing food. I once found a four-foot long snakeskin hanging from a tree cavity. Guess who lived *there*?

A winter tree often keeps another secret—its own identity. It can be tricky to identify a tree without leaves, fruit, flowers, or seeds to help you. In winter, you have to look at a tree's characteristic shape and size and pattern of branching. (*See "Look at a Tree's Bare Bones" on page 49 of* A Kid's Fall EcoJournal.) You can learn to recognize trees by their buds, seed pods, or bark, too.

Each species of tree has a different bark, which covers and protects the tree trunk. As the trunk grows, the bark stretches and cracks. It peels, splits, or forms deep furrows. You can record these patterns by making a collection of bark rubbings. All you need are paper and a dark colored crayon. Peel the paper off the crayon. Put the paper against the trunk of a tree and then rub the side of the crayon back and forth over the paper. The texture of the bark will show up. You can gather loose or fallen bark to keep with the bark rubbings, but don't peel healthy bark from the tree.

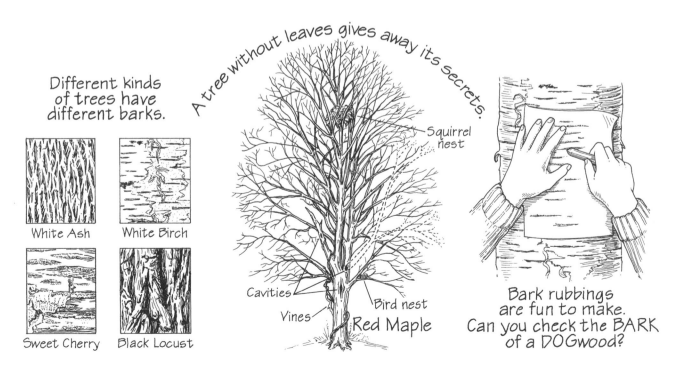

Different kinds of trees have different barks.

White Ash

White Birch

Sweet Cherry

Black Locust

A tree without leaves gives away its secrets.

Squirrel nest

Cavities

Vines

Bird nest

Red Maple

Bark rubbings are fun to make. Can you check the BARK of a DOGwood?

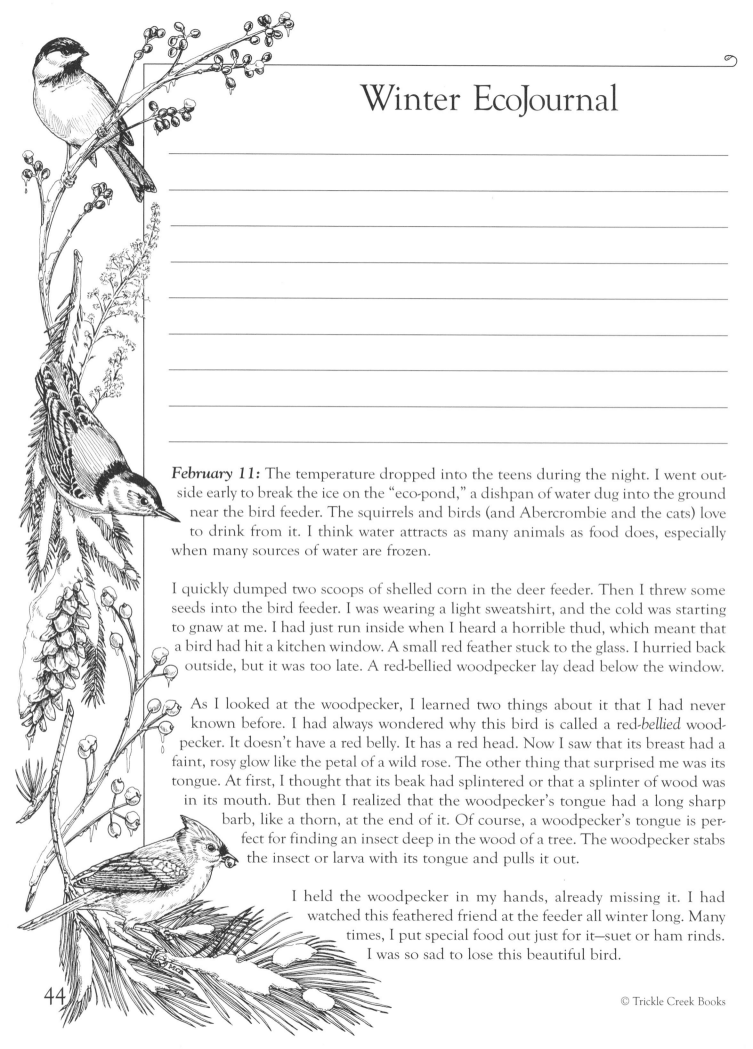

Winter EcoJournal

February 11: The temperature dropped into the teens during the night. I went outside early to break the ice on the "eco-pond," a dishpan of water dug into the ground near the bird feeder. The squirrels and birds (and Abercrombie and the cats) love to drink from it. I think water attracts as many animals as food does, especially when many sources of water are frozen.

I quickly dumped two scoops of shelled corn in the deer feeder. Then I threw some seeds into the bird feeder. I was wearing a light sweatshirt, and the cold was starting to gnaw at me. I had just run inside when I heard a horrible thud, which meant that a bird had hit a kitchen window. A small red feather stuck to the glass. I hurried back outside, but it was too late. A red-bellied woodpecker lay dead below the window.

As I looked at the woodpecker, I learned two things about it that I had never known before. I had always wondered why this bird is called a red-*bellied* woodpecker. It doesn't have a red belly. It has a red head. Now I saw that its breast had a faint, rosy glow like the petal of a wild rose. The other thing that surprised me was its tongue. At first, I thought that its beak had splintered or that a splinter of wood was in its mouth. But then I realized that the woodpecker's tongue had a long sharp barb, like a thorn, at the end of it. Of course, a woodpecker's tongue is perfect for finding an insect deep in the wood of a tree. The woodpecker stabs the insect or larva with its tongue and pulls it out.

I held the woodpecker in my hands, already missing it. I had watched this feathered friend at the feeder all winter long. Many times, I put special food out just for it—suet or ham rinds. I was so sad to lose this beautiful bird.

Birds Can't Talk—Or Can They?

Wouldn't it be interesting if you could take a poll to find out exactly what birds like to eat at your feeder? Of course, birds can't respond by writing or talking, but they can certainly tell you their preferences. You might like to set up an experiment that will be as good as a poll.

Collect several disposable plastic containers, such as small margarine tubs. Nail the containers to a board, leaving enough space between the containers for birds to land. Fill each container with a different kind of bird food, such as sunflower seeds, cracked corn, nuts, chopped fruit, suet, or small birdseed. Fill one container with water, and try to keep the water from freezing solid. Remove ice from the surface and add more water as often as you can. Use a marker to label each container, so that you can remember what it contained after it is empty. Place the board with the containers of food on a picnic table or a stump or directly on the ground. Then watch!

There are several things to observe in this experiment. Watch how much food is left in each container. Then you can easily tell which kinds of food are most popular with your winter birds. Spend some time watching one container of food to see which birds eat that food. Watch one bird at a time to see if it will try more than one kind of food. Watch the container with water. How many of the birds that come to the feeder drink water? Are more birds attracted to the water on frozen days when puddles and ponds have turned to ice?

To really learn something about wild birds, keep a written record of your observations. Include the date, the time of day, and notes about the weather. The best times to observe birds feeding is in the morning and evening. Many feeders are deserted during the middle of the day while birds rest. If you devote ten or fifteen minutes a day to careful observation, you'll be amazed at how much you learn—and laugh—and like being a birdwatcher.

When you set up an experiment with bird food, you never know what results you might get!

Gray squirrel · Downy woodpecker · Blue jay · Wild turkey · Cardinal

CHOPPED NUTS · SUNFLOWER SEEDS · SUET · CRACKED CORN · WATER · SMALL BIRDSEED · CHOPPED FRUIT

Winter EcoJournal

_____

_____

_____

_____

_____

_____

_____

_____

_____

_____

February 15: There is nothing as discouraging as a February blizzard. Just when we are tiring of winter and longing for spring, a cold, howling wind dumped mounds of snow on us. It snowed all night and all day. The pine trees are bowed down with heavy heaps of snow on every branch. Even leafless trees are weighted with snow. The snow comes down like fluffy popcorn spilling from a huge white bowl. Huge, wet snowflakes (popcorn balls) splat against the windows.

The snow piled up on every surface, including electrical lines. At dusk, our lights went off. Without electricity, we had no light, heat, or water. Our water comes from a well, but we need electricity to run the pump. Our house is heated by burning logs in a wood-burning furnace, but we need electricity to force the hot air through ductwork into every room. I rounded up candles and flashlights while Bob built a fire in the fireplace in our family room. Before darkness fell, we brought everything into the room that we would need for the evening—food, books, pillows and blankets. Charlie was already sleeping on a little sofa, which he thinks is his. Abercrombie settled on a rug in front of the fire, where dogs have slept throughout history. And Bailey sat boldly on the hearth. We were ready to "tough it out."

At first, we were busy warming soup and cooking hotdogs on the fire. (Abercrombie ate two!) Then we read for awhile by firelight and candlelight. The wind howled, the popcorn snow splatted, the night grew darker, and the house grew colder. We snuggled under piles of blankets and went to sleep at 6:30 p.m. What else could we do? We woke four hours later when the lights came back on.

46

Fire-Baked Apples and Octopus Dogs

Have you ever sat by a campfire on a warm summer night, listening to the rhythm of insect songs and toasting marshmallows? You have? Well, have you ever crouched close to a campfire on a frozen winter night, watching the stars a million miles away through bare and leafless branches? The crackling heat from a winter campfire is perfect for warming numb hands and feet. And hot food cooked over the flames or in the coals is the best tasting stuff in the world!

To cook hot dogs (or spicy sausages), cut a slit down the length of the hot dog. Then use a long-handled fork or a green stick sharpened at one end to hold the hot dog over the flames of the fire. Cook the hot dog until it is brown and puffy. Remove it from the fire and put a slice of cheese inside the slit in the hot dog. The cheese will melt while you toast a hot dog bun over the fire. Add ketchup, mustard, relish, onions, or whatever you like. Hmmm!

If you'd like to eat something funny, make an octopus dog by making eight long cuts in a hot dog, beginning about an inch from one end of the hot dog. Insert the cooking fork or sharp stick into the end of the hot dog that isn't cut. As you cook the octopus dog, its eight "legs" will curl up and look silly—but it will taste great!

Another campfire treat is fire-baked apples. Wash each apple and then use a metal spoon to dig out most of its core. Don't go all the way through the apple. Fill the opening with butter, sugar, and cinnamon. Then wrap the apples in foil and carefully place them in the coals of a fire. Bake the apples in the coals for half an hour or more until they are tender. Remove them from the fire, un-wrap them, and let them cool a little before eating them. (*Note:* Ask an adult to help you get the apples in and out of the fire. Even after the apples are unwrapped, the sugar will be hot enough to burn you, so be careful!)

Octopus dogs are good to eat when you get past the wiggles and giggles.

If you have a fireplace, fire-baked apples (octopus dogs, too) can be cooked inside.

Winter EcoJournal

_____

_____

_____

_____

_____

_____

_____

_____

_____

_____

_____

_____

_____

_____

February 16: The blizzard is over. The sky is a thin, milky blue. The sun is shining, and the snow is dazzling. I thought I was tired of snow, but I have to admit that this fresh snowfall is too beautiful to describe. I made my way down to the creek, which wasn't easy in a foot of snow. The sound of rushing water was wonderful. The water was a transparent green, and I could clearly see little colored pebbles, black, brown, and orange, on the bottom.

I used a branch to brush the snow off a fallen log, so that I could sit on it. Beneath the snow, the log was covered with fresh, green moss. It was such a bright green—a spring green—that I stared at it in delight. Then I wondered if there were any more green to be found in the frozen white world around me. I dug under the snow along the creek bank. Wet, sticky balls of snow clung to my mittens, but I didn't care, because I was uncovering green grass. I found something else, too. A mole tunnel. The mole hadn't dug the tunnel under the ground. The shallow, bottom half of the tunnel was scooped out of the dirt, but the top half of the tunnel was snow. There were other tunnels and runways at the bottom of the snow. It gave me a rare glimpse of the cozy, undersnow world where little mammals (moles, voles, mice, and shrews) stay active during the winter.

48

Under the Snow

Have you ever heard someone talk about a "blanket" of snow on the ground? That's a very accurate description, because snow contains so much air that it is a fine *insulator*. Snow feels cold to the touch, but a layer of snow is like a blanket. It actually keeps everything below the snow warmer, because it keeps heat from escaping.

Late in winter, after several snowfalls, it is interesting to dig under the snow to see what is there. Choose a flat place to work. (If you dig snow on the side of a hill or mountain—even in the woods—you could cause a dangerous avalanche, or swift snowslide.) Use a snow shovel, a trowel, or your hands to remove an area of snow. Stand in the open area that you make, and carefully "slice" through the snow at one side, so that you can see from the top to the bottom of the snow. Can you date the major snowfalls from earliest to latest? Can you measure the amount of each snowfall? While you're observing the area, test the ground to see if it is frozen. Is it hard to embed a trowel in the earth? Is the ground dry and crunchy under your feet?

Look at the area that you have cleared of snow. Do you see green grass, green moss, or even green plants and flowers? Are there signs of nests or burrows? Sort through the leaf litter about eight inches from the trunk of a tree, especially in the angle of the roots. Dig down an inch or two to look for wintering pupae of moths and other insects. (A *pupa* is an insect in the stage between larva and adult. The pupa of a moth is wrapped in a cocoon.) Can you find a hibernating snail? After observing pupae or other tiny creatures, replace the dirt and leaf litter that covered them.

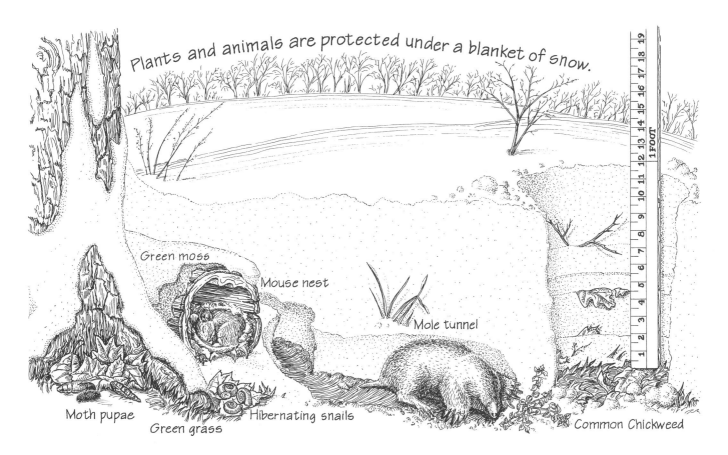

Plants and animals are protected under a blanket of snow.

Green moss

Mouse nest

Mole tunnel

Moth pupae

Green grass

Hibernating snails

Common Chickweed

Winter EcoJournal

_____
_____
_____
_____
_____
_____
_____
_____
_____
_____
_____
_____
_____
_____
_____
_____
_____

February 20: The squirrels know that winter is yielding to spring. The gray squirrels are fast and frisky, chasing each other up and down tall trees. A pair of tiny red squirrels are so quick that we can hardly follow them with our eyes. They run out to the very end of a branch and leap through the air to another tree. Then down and up and over and through the air, one behind the other.

Two clever gray squirrels have made a winter home in one of the hollow columns that supports the roof over our deck. They enter at the top of the twenty-foot column and go down inside it to the very bottom. This morning, we watched them beginning to nest. One squirrel seemed to be stationed at the top as a lookout—or maybe as the supervisor. The other would gather a great mouthful of leaves, run up the pine tree, and leap to the top of the column. What a cozy leaf nest they must be building deep down inside the column. The cats know the squirrels are inside. They have thoroughly investigated the bottom of the column, but the squirrels are safe from any intruder.

50

Squirrels Eat, Too

Many people spend a great deal of time, energy, and money trying to keep squirrels from eating at bird feeders. I don't know why. Squirrels and birds eat side by side at our feeder. Squirrels don't chase the birds away, and they don't eat all of the birdseed. They are so much fun to watch and to get to know. In spring and early summer, when the baby squirrels start coming to the feeder, it's like a circus coming to town!

At the bird-and-squirrel feeder, we put out birdseed, sunflower seeds, and shelled corn. Squirrels like corn and sunflower seeds best. They also eat nuts, of course. In the fall, I pick up acorns and hickory nuts to put in the feeder. During the long winter, we serve them dried corn on the cob at feeders of their own.

You can easily make a squirrel feeder by driving 16-penny nails through a small board, 1"x 4"x18". (To prevent the board from splitting, predrill holes for the nails with a $\frac{1}{8}$-inch drill bit.) Then use three #10x2 wood screws to attach the board to a post about four feet long. Buy corn at a feed mill or garden center, push an ear of corn firmly down on each nail, and watch the squirrels come to dine!

Another way to feed squirrels is to make a corn basket. Use wire cutters to cut a six-foot length of 8-gauge wire into three lengths. (Cut two lengths 22" long and one length 26" long.) Bend the two 22-inch pieces of wire into support loops. Bend the third length of wire into a support for the basket lid. Use chicken mesh with 2-inch openings to form the basket, the bottom of the basket, and the lid. Cut the mesh so that you can wrap the wire ends around the support loops and the lid support with pliers. Use a hammer to attach the lid to a 1"x8"x18" board with $\frac{1}{2}$" wire staples. Also attach the basket to the board with wire staples. Attach two screw eyes to the back of the board, one near each long edge, about six inches from the top edge of the board. Secure the corn basket to a tree with a bungee cord. Fill the basket with dried corn on the cob and see how fast the squirrels empty it.

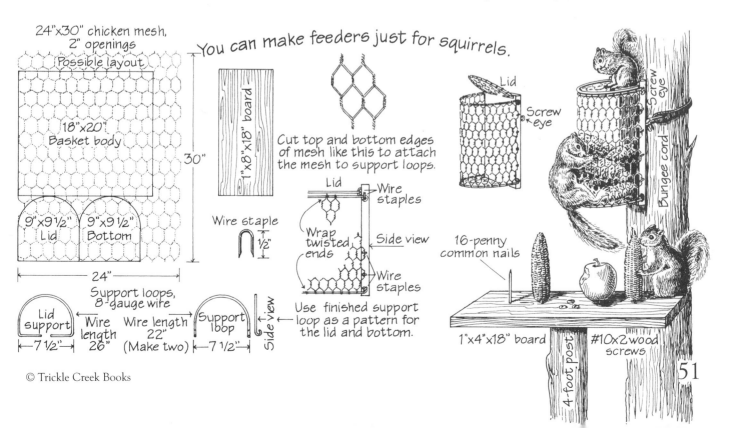

24"x30" chicken mesh, 2" openings

Possible layout

18"x20" Basket body

30"

9"x9½" Lid

9"x9½" Bottom

24"

Support loops, 8-gauge wire

Lid support

7½"

Wire length 26"

Wire length 22" (Make two)

Support loop

7½"

Side view

You can make feeders just for squirrels.

1"x8"x18" board

Wire staple

½"

Cut top and bottom edges of mesh like this to attach the mesh to support loops.

Lid

Wire staples

Wrap twisted ends

Side view

Wire staples

Use finished support loop as a pattern for the lid and bottom.

Lid

Screw eye

Screw eye

Bungee cord

16-penny common nails

1"x4"x18" board

4-foot post

#10x2 wood screws

51

Winter EcoJournal

February 28: It is the end of February. There are faint promises of spring. The light is different. The sun is a little higher in the sky. The air and the earth are warming up. The creeks are running hard, full of melted snow. Water runs across the road and over rocks and along animal trails in the woods. Trickle Creek is exuberant, splashing over its narrow banks. The leafless trees stand patiently waiting for a call to action.

One of these days, some mysterious signal will be given, and the sleeping seeds and the sleeping buds will burst open and birds will sing and little animals will be born. Nature will wake up with a shout of joy, refreshed and renewed after the long, quiet sleep of winter.

My heart sings just thinking about it!

52

Celebrate Winter

Build a snowman or a snow animal!

Catch snowflakes on your tongue.

Lie down in the snow and make a snow angel.

Break the ice on a puddle and listen to it crack!

Give a winter treat to a friend.

Winter Food for Wild Birds

If you really want to help wild birds survive the winter, you need to provide a variety of rich, high-energy foods for them. The chart below will help you decide which foods to put in your bird feeder. You can choose special treats for the birds that already come to your feeder. Or you can try to attract new birds by putting out their favorite foods. *Note:* The foods listed on the chart are good for feeding adult birds during the winter. In spring and summer, there are plenty of natural foods that are better for young birds.

Wild Birds	Favorite Foods
Blue jays, chickadees, flickers, grackles, nuthatches, red-winged blackbirds, starlings, tufted titmice, woodpeckers	Suet, bacon grease
Blue jays, cardinals, chickadees, goldfinches, grackles, grosbeaks, juncos, nuthatches, purple finches, tufted titmice, woodpeckers	Sunflower seeds
Blue jays, brown thrashers, cardinals, Carolina wrens, chickadees, juncos, purple finches, sparrows, starlings, tufted titmice	Greasy crusts and crumbs, doughnuts
Brown thrashers, cardinals, chickadees, cowbirds, goldfinches, grackles, hermit thrushes, juncos, mourning doves, pine grosbeaks, pine siskins, purple finches, redpolls, sparrows	Small birdseed, such as millet, canary seed, chicken feed, and cracked corn
Blue jays, bob-whites, crows, grackles, mourning doves, pheasants, ruffed grouse, starlings, wild turkey	Large birdseed, such as sunflower seeds, wheat, oats, corn, buckwheat, and soybean
Blue jays, cardinals, chickadees, finches, flickers, grosbeaks, nuthatches, sparrows, tufted titmice, woodpeckers	Peanut butter, nuts
Bluebirds, cardinals, Carolina wrens, cedar waxwings, hermit thrushes, mockingbirds, starlings, thrashers, woodpeckers	Fruits, such as chopped apples, bananas, and raisins

Conifers and Cones

In winter, when most of the landscape is black and white and gray, how we love the evergreens! The evergreens are colorful and fragrant while other trees are sleeping through a quiet, frozen season. They provide both food and shelter for birds and animals. It is pure pleasure to rest our eyes on a dark green spruce with its limbs gracefully curving up to welcome falling snow. Or to admire a long-needled white pine with snow-laden limbs drooping to the ground. Or to look up at a lacy hemlock towering high above our heads.

Most *conifers* are evergreens that bear cones. (There are a few exceptions. Some conifers, such as larches, drop their needles in fall. And some conifers, such as red cedars, don't have true cones. They have fruits or berries.) If all "Christmas trees" look alike to you, you will enjoy sharpening your observation skills by learning to identify some of the conifers. Look closely at their cones, too, because every tree has its own kind of cone.

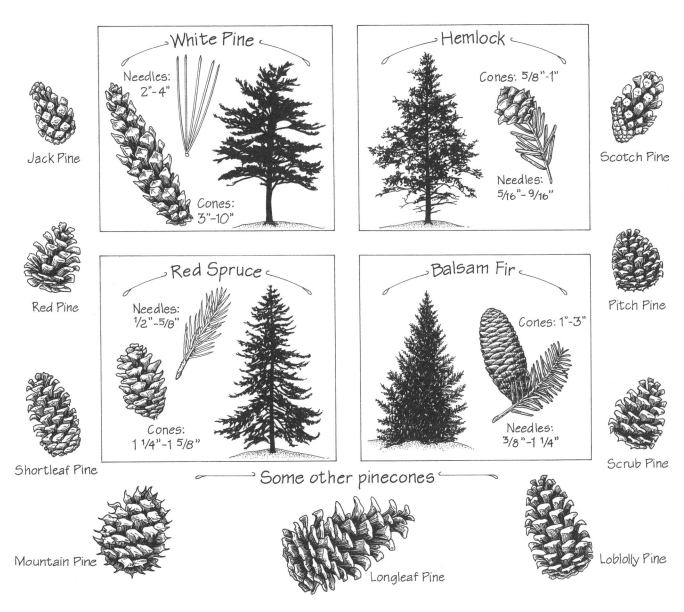

Jack Pine

White Pine
Needles: 2"- 4"
Cones: 3"-10"

Hemlock
Cones: 5/8"-1"
Needles: 5/16"- 9/16"

Scotch Pine

Red Pine

Red Spruce
Needles: 1/2"-5/8"
Cones: 1 1/4"-1 5/8"

Balsam Fir
Cones: 1"-3"
Needles: 3/8"-1 1/4"

Pitch Pine

Shortleaf Pine

Scrub Pine

Some other pinecones

Mountain Pine

Longleaf Pine

Loblolly Pine

An EcoJournal for Every Season

You'll want to own all four of them.

Trickle Creek Books offers a series of four EcoJournals, one for each season, which are written by Toni Albert and illustrated by Margaret Brandt. All of the EcoJournals invite kids to explore the seasons with unusual nature activities and then to write about their experiences. The books include exquisitely illustrated writing pages for children, short entries from the author's nature journals that reflect her irrepressible delight in the natural world, and dozens of nature activities for children to try. Kids learn to develop a deep love and respect for the environment.

Here are some of the activities that are found in the other EcoJournals:

A Kid's Spring EcoJournal

- Build a mole dome
- Make a track trap
- Raise a wild caterpillar or tadpoles
- Build an eco-pond
- Make wildflower crafts
- Plant a butterfly garden
- Build a wildlife blind

A Kid's Summer EcoJournal

- Build a turtle platform
- Grow a birdhouse
- Make a mushroom spore print
- Attract moths with a "shining sheet"
- Create a sun print
- Make a creek aquarium

A Kid's Fall EcoJournal

- Collect leaf galls and raise the larvae
- Build a bat house
- Collect a spider web
- Dissect an owl pellet
- Make leaf prints
- Sprout an acorn
- Take a sock walk

Each EcoJournal sells for $9.95. Order from your bookseller, online bookseller, or directly from us.

Trickle Creek Books

500 Andersontown Road
Mechanicsburg, PA 17055-6055

Toll-free 24-hour telephone - 800-353-2791
Telephone - 717-766-2638 • **Fax** - 717-766-1343
Web site - www.TrickleCreekBooks.com • **E-mail** - tonialbert@aol.com

Satisfaction Guarantee - If you are not satisfied with your purchase for any reason, return books for full refund. Thanks for ordering.